The
ITALIAN
VEGETABLE
COOKBOOK

The
ITALIAN
VEGETABLE
COOKBOOK

200 Favorite Recipes for Antipasti,
Soups, Pasta, Main Dishes,
and Desserts

MICHELE SCICOLONE

Photographs by Alan Richardson

A RUX MARTIN BOOK

HOUGHTON MIFFLIN HARCOURT

Boston   New York   2014

For information about permission to reproduce selections
from this book, write to Permissions, Houghton Mifflin
Harcourt Publishing Company, 215 Park Avenue South,
New York, New York 10003.

www.hmhco.com

Library of Congress Cataloging-in-Publication Data
Scicolone, Michele, author.
 The Italian vegetable cookbook : 200 favorite recipes for
antipasti, soups, pasta, main dishes, and desserts / Michele
Scicolone ; photographs by Alan Richardson..
    pages cm
 "A Rux Martin book."
   ISBN 978-0-547-90916-5 (hardback); 978-0-547-91064-2 (ebk)
1. Cooking, Italian. 2. Cooking (Vegetables) I. Title.
 TX723.S36635 2014
 641.5945—dc23

                              2013044247

Book design by Casandra Pappas

Food styling by Karen Tack

Prop styling by Deb Donahue

Printed in the United States

DOW 10 9 8 7 6 5 4 3 2 1

To Charles

Acknowledgments

Whenever I finish a new cookbook, someone invariably asks me how long it took me to write it. For this book, I would have to say that it has taken a lifetime. Many of the recipes are traditional ones that I grew up eating every day. I learned them by watching and cooking with my mother, grandmothers, relatives, and family friends. When I was older, other cooks inspired and taught me. I traveled in Italy, taking photos and making notes. I ate at friends' homes and in restaurants, talked with produce vendors, chefs, and home cooks, visited growers and food producers, and read books and magazines on Italian cooking and even gardening. All of those experiences became a part of this book.

My thanks to all of those who have helped and taught and inspired me in so many different ways. I hope that this book will do the same for those who browse its pages.

Thank you to the great team at Houghton Mifflin Harcourt who contribute so much. Rux Martin, my editor, knows just what is needed to make my work so much better. Her appreciation, encouragement, and good humor mean a lot to me.

Photographer Alan Richardson always seems to know how to capture my feelings and express my ideas about Italian food with his evocative photos. It was a pleasure to work with him. And again, Karen Tack and Deb Donahue brought their creativity and style to the food and props.

Judith Sutton can always be relied upon for her careful reading of my work and thoughtful suggestions.

My grateful appreciation to Judith Weber, my agent and longtime friend, for years of good advice and sharing countless great meals.

Thank you to my husband, Charles, for all of his help, patience, and lots of good wine.

Contents

Introduction

"What was the best thing you ate?" friends often ask me when I return from Italy. The answer they expect is something like silken pasta handmade by a smiling *nonna* in her farmhouse kitchen, or perhaps a dreamy new flavor of ice cream from a sleek Milanese *gelateria*. So, after a recent trip, no one was quite ready for me to rave about eggplant.

"You had a whole meal of eggplant?" one incredulous friend asked as I described a dinner that began with crispy eggplant cutlets served with a roasted tomato sauce, followed by pasta with eggplant and tomato almond pesto and, finally, eggplant towers oozing milky fresh mozzarella. I tried to explain how flavorful and satisfying everything was, but I don't think she will believe me until she can taste these dishes herself.

Vegetables and fruits have always been at the heart of Italian cooking. That's why when you visit an Italian neighborhood in this country, you often see vegetable gardens growing on every available patch of soil. Whether it is a fig tree in the backyard, tomatoes in a window box, or basil in a planter on the front porch, all are tended with loving care. In season and freshly picked, the fruits and vegetables are all the more delicious as a result.

In our small backyard in Brooklyn, my mother managed to coax tomatoes, cantaloupes, zucchini, and basil out of a tiny patch of earth surrounded by a sea of concrete. Each year she carefully preserved seeds from her summer harvest to plant the following summer.

On my first visit to Italy, as we drove from the airport to our hotel, I noticed little swatches of peppers, zucchini, and artichokes everywhere, even on the highway median strips. In cities and towns, tomatoes and basil flourished in recycled olive oil cans on terraces and window balconies. Fig, lemon, and peach trees abounded in front and backyards, bay and rosemary bushes lined the walks in the public parks, and blackberries thrived along country roads. Olive, pomegranate, and walnut trees shaded public squares, available for all to enjoy.

Because Italy was historically a poor country, eating meat was reserved mostly for special occasions. Fish, which might have been easy to catch, was more often sold than eaten. Since the country is blessed with fertile land and a long growing season (at least in Southern Italy), the most readily available foods have always been the fresh fruits, grains, legumes, herbs, nuts, and vegetables found growing wild or cultivated in even the smallest plots.

Resourceful cooks learned how to handle thorny nettles and tough cardoons. They cooked wild greens in soups or turned them into sauces or stews to top polenta or pasta. Fruits at their peak of flavor but on the verge of being overripe were transformed into jams, sauces, or tarts. With such a bounty of produce, all a good cook needed to add was a bit of creativity. And whether it comes to music, art, or cooking, Italians have never lacked for that.

In this book, I wanted to share some of the mouthwatering dishes I have tasted in my years of traveling through Italy. Many of the recipes were given to me by talented home cooks. I tasted other dishes in restaurants or gleaned them from the Italian cooking magazines and cookbooks I collect. Still other recipes were handed down by my grandparents, who came from the Naples area, or by my husband's family, who were from Sicily. Traditional dishes like stuffed artichokes, sautéed mushrooms, and spinach (or other greens) with garlic and hot pepper taste as good today as they did when my mother made them for our family many years ago.

The recipes in this book all feature vegetables, grains, or fruits in some form, but you will notice that some contain small amounts of pancetta or anchovies, or suggest chicken broth as an alternative ingredient. Because I eat mostly vegetables but am not a vegetarian, I sometimes use these ingredients as a seasoning, the way Italians do. If you prefer to omit them, by all means do so. You can always amp up the flavor by adding a handful of olives, herbs, red pepper, or some chopped capers—whatever works best with the recipe.

Whether you are eliminating meat and fish from your diet, trying to introduce the occasional Meatless Monday, or just looking for new vegetable and fruit recipes to add to your repertoire, you will find lots of great choices in these pages. A handful of ingredients and a bit of time are all it takes to make a simple, satisfying meal. For example, for Orecchiette with Potatoes and Arugula, the potatoes and pasta cook in the same pot, the arugula is added, and they are then tossed with garlic and hot pepper. Radicchio and Grape Salad, perhaps accompanied with a wedge of fontina cheese, would be a perfect ending to this supper. Too hot to use the stove? Turn to Cold Cucumber Cream with Tomato Salsa, a delectable soup that requires no cooking. Follow that with Peach, Tomato, and Burrata Salad, and you have a meal that will leave you feeling refreshed.

Other recipes are so hearty that no one will even notice that they don't include meat. See Sofia's Eggplant-Rice Timbale, which consists of rice, eggplant, tomato sauce, and cheese baked in a casserole. Got leftover pasta? Mix it—any kind will do—with eggs,

cooked vegetables, and cheese and bake it into a Pasta Torta. The result is so good you can serve it to company.

Italian holiday meals are often meatless. The double-crusted Easter Swiss Chard and Ricotta Pie, filled with ricotta, chard, and Parmesan, is ideal for a spring brunch. Serve it with Grilled Vegetables with Herb Dressing and finish the meal with a spectacular Two-Berry Tiramisu, layers of cream, sweet berries, and ladyfingers. Peach Cremolata alla Panna (with whipped cream) is a traditional Roman dessert that I make each year when blushing peaches are at their best and dripping with juice. On the lighter side, try the sophisticated Pear and Grappa Sorbet.

While Italians have devised countless techniques for preparing vegetables, none are difficult. Even those new to cooking will find plenty of uncomplicated recipes in this book. Italian cooks are not bound by strict rules, and you should feel free to use whatever vegetables or fruits look their best. If that means using collard greens instead of escarole, or adding watercress to a salad instead of arugula, or substituting ripe mangoes for peaches, go right ahead. Certain frozen vegetables can be a good alternative when you don't have a chance to get to the market. Choosing what works at the moment is in the spirit of Italian cooking and will always result in the best food on your table.

Storing Vegetables and Fruits

Whether you buy your vegetables and fruits at the local farmers' market or at the supermarket, the following tips will help you keep them fresh.

- Vegetables and fruits need to breathe, so poke holes in their plastic bags before refrigerating them.
- Store vegetables and fruits in separate drawers—some fruits, such as apples, release gases that can cause vegetables and other fruits to become overripe.
- Remove rubber bands or ties, which can create bruising, from vegetables like spinach or broccoli.
- Wash leafy greens just before you are ready to use them. First look them over and discard any wilted, bruised, or yellowing leaves or parts. Place the greens in a sink filled with cool water, swirling the greens, and wait a bit to allow any grit to sink to the bottom. Lift out the greens, drain and rinse out the sink, and add fresh water, then repeat until there are no traces of grit left in the sink. Three times is usually about right. You can also rinse in a salad spinner.
- Some fruits are best kept at room temperature rather than in the refrigerator. These include tomatoes, bananas, pears, apples, melons, peaches, plums, and apricots. They will continue to ripen at room temperature and should be eaten or refrigerated once ripe. (Tomatoes, however, should never be refrigerated.)
- Fruits such as berries, cherries, grapes, figs, and citrus should be refrigerated because they will ripen rapidly at room temperature and can spoil. If they are too cold when you are ready to eat them, put them in warm water for a few minutes to bring out their flavor.
- Recently a number of products that claim to wash produce more thoroughly than just water have appeared on the market. None are worth the expense. But for extra protection against 98 percent of bacteria, you can spray whole vegetables and fruits with a mix of 1 part white vinegar to 3 parts fresh water. Keep the spray bottle near the sink, rinse the sprayed fruit or vegetables thoroughly to eliminate any vinegar taste, and dry with a clean dish towel or paper towels.

Apples

Apples can go from crisp to mushy quickly, so it is best to store them in the crisper in plastic bags with holes in them; keep them separate from vegetables and other fruits because of the gases they release (see above). Alternatively, to accelerate the ripening of peaches or bananas, store them in a bag with an apple or two. Wash apples just before using.

Asparagus

When buying asparagus, look for closed tips and crisp stems. Store them in the refrigerator, standing up in a bowl with an inch or two of cool water. When you are ready to cook it, rinse well in cool water. Trim off the stem ends at the point where the color turns from green to white.

For extra tenderness, you can peel thick asparagus before cooking, though I generally don't bother. To peel, lay a spear on a cutting board and peel from below the tip to the stem end with a knife or a vegetable peeler. Turn the spear and continue all around. Thin asparagus does not need to be peeled.

Some cooks prefer thick asparagus, while others look for thin stalks. I think they are both good.

Berries

Strawberries, blueberries, blackberries, and raspberries should be brightly colored and dry-looking. Moisture can encourage the growth of mold, so keep them dry and cool until you are ready to eat them. Even a small spot of mold can spread quickly and spoil a whole box of berries.

To store berries, lay a paper towel on a dinner plate and scatter the berries on it so that they are not crowded together; cover them lightly and refrigerate. When you're ready to use them, place the berries in a strainer and rinse them gently with a spray of cool water. If they are very dirty, you can place the strainer in a large bowl of water (I use the strainer and bowl of my salad spinner) and give them a quick swirl, but don't let them soak and absorb water. Shake the strainer gently or spin the berries to remove the excess water. Pat dry with paper towels.

Broccoli, Broccoli Rabe, and Cauliflower

Look for dark green bunches of broccoli, with no sign of yellowing. The stalks and any leaves should be crisp. Romanesco broccoli is a pale green variety whose head resembles a cluster of seashells. It has a mild flavor that is closer to cauliflower than broccoli.

Broccolini, a variety of broccoli developed in Japan in the 1990s, looks like a junior form of broccoli, with slender stems and smaller heads. The flavor is mild. It can be cooked just like broccoli.

Broccoli rabe, sometimes spelled raab or rape (pronounced *rah*-peh) or called rapini, has longer, narrower stems, more leaves, and smaller heads than regular broccoli. Sometimes you will see small yellow flowers; if there are a lot of these, the vegetable is probably too mature.

Cauliflower can be creamy white, orange, or purple. Look for clean heads with no bruises or browning.

To prepare members of the broccoli family for cooking, trim off the base of the stems, core cauliflower, and rinse in cool water.

Brussels Sprouts

Brussels sprouts look like miniature cabbages, and in fact, they are a member of the same family of cruciferous vegetables. The freshest Brussels sprouts are green and white, with no yellowing or dark spots.

To prepare Brussels sprouts for cooking, rinse them in cool water. With a sharp knife, trim the base of each one.

Carrots

Carrots can be orange, yellow, white, or red. Buy carrots with stems on for freshness; both the stems and carrots should be fresh- and crisp-looking. At home, cut off all but one inch of the tops and store in the crisper in a plastic bag with holes poked in it. Precut carrots (so-called baby carrots) are just mature carrots cut small. They lack flavor and are sometimes treated with preservatives. I avoid them.

Cherries

Look for shiny, dark-colored red cherries with fresh green stems. Yellow Rainier cherries should be glossy and plump-looking. Store cherries in the refrigerator and wash in cool water just before serving.

Citrus Fruits

Oranges, lemons, clementines, and other citrus fruits should have shiny skins and a bright color, with no bruises, and feel heavy for their size. Brownish speckles on the skins of grapefruits and oranges are actually an indication of sweetness and good flavor. Citrus fruits should be stored loose in the crisper drawer of the refrigerator.

Eggplants

Eggplants can be big or small, long or round, purple, white, or striped, but regardless of their appearance, their flavor is pretty much the same. At one time, eggplants were always salted before cooking to draw out the bitter juices, but newer strains have been developed that do not require this step.

Look for firm eggplants with taut skin, green tops, and no rusty brown spots.

Fennel

Often mislabeled anise, fennel has a white bulb, green stems that resemble celery ribs, and fine pale green fronds. It has a mild licorice flavor and can be eaten raw or cooked.

Look for bulbs with no bruises or brown spots. Trim off the base of the bulb and remove the green stems before using.

Figs

Figs can be green, brown, black, or striped. Ripe figs spoil quickly, so look for fully ripe fruits and use them as soon as possible. They should be plump and soft. Italians like them best when there is a "teardrop in the eye"—a drop of nectar in the flower end of the fruit that indicates the perfect state of ripeness. White or grayish spots on the skin are an indication of mold, and such figs should be avoided. Don't wash them until just before using. Italians often peel figs before eating them, but that is not necessary.

Green Beans

Look for beans that are deep green and crisp, with no bruises. Yellow or wax beans can be substituted for the green, since their flavor is very similar. Buy beans that are all about the same size so that they will cook evenly. Store them loosely wrapped in a plastic bag with holes poked in it in the refrigerator. Remove the stem end before cooking.

Leafy Greens

Spinach, Swiss chard, beet greens, kale, escarole, lettuce, chicory, arugula, dandelion, nettles, and puntarelle are just a few of the leafy greens, both wild and cultivated, favored by Italian cooks. The handling and cooking methods are much the same for all of them, so use whatever looks best and is in season, adjusting the cooking time as needed.

Store greens in a plastic bag with holes in it in the refrigerator. Wash them well before using to eliminate any grit.

Mushrooms

Mushrooms should be kept dry and stored loosely wrapped in a paper bag in the refrigerator. Wash them just before cooking. If they are relatively clean, you can simply wipe them off with a damp paper towel. Wash dirtier fungi the same way as berries (see page 6).

Onions, Leeks, Scallions, and Garlic

Yellow onions are usually my first choice for cooking, but when I want a sweeter, milder onion for salads or certain recipes, I often use red onions. Cipollini, small onions that look slightly flattened, are good for cooking whole. If you can't find cipollini, pearl onions are a good substitute.

Onions should be dry, with no bruises or sprouting. When buying onions packed in a mesh bag, use your nose—you may not be able to see inside the bag to tell whether the onions are spoiled, but you will certainly be able to smell spoilage. Onions can be stored in a dark, cool, dry place or in the refrigerator—whichever is more convenient.

To reduce the strength of the flavor of onions, slice or chop them, then soak them in cold water for 30 minutes, changing the water once or twice. Drain and pat dry before using.

Don't let onions turn dark brown when sautéing them, or they will be bitter. If necessary, add a couple of tablespoons of water and lower the heat.

Scallions, also known as green onions, are either immature regular onions or a variety of onion that does not form big bulbs. They should be stored loosely wrapped in paper towels in the crisper drawer of the refrigerator. To prepare them for cooking, slice off the root end and 2 or 3 inches of green at the tops.

Leeks look like giant scallions, but they have a tougher texture. Store them loosely wrapped in paper towels in the refrigerator. Trim off the root ends and most of the green tops before using. Leeks can be very sandy inside, so cut them lengthwise in half and wash them well in between the layers.

Fresh garlic is mild and sweet-tasting; look for plump heads with no traces of bruising or yellowing. The skin should look pearly and be attached to the cloves.

To peel a garlic clove, place it on a cutting board and lay the flat side of a heavy chef's knife against it. Smack the knife with the heel of your hand to partially smash the garlic and crack open the skin. Cut off the end of the clove and remove the skin. Depending on the effect you want, garlic can be left whole, sliced, or chopped.

Where you want just a hint of garlic for sauces or dressings, use the peeled and lightly crushed clove. After the cooking or marinating, you can easily remove it before serving the dish. If you want more of a garlic presence in the dish, thinly slice or very finely chop the garlic. When sautéing, be careful not to let the finely cut garlic overcook and turn brown, or its flavor will be bitter. When you want the garlic to blend in completely, as in a stuffing or meatball mixture, grate the cloves on a Microplane grater (watch your fingers!). It does a great job and makes cleanup easy.

Pears

Pears range from pale green to yellow to brown or red, depending on the variety, and at least one variety or another is in season year-round. Pears should have smooth, firm skin with no blemishes. It's always best to buy fruits that are slightly underripe and allow them to ripen at room temperature. Pears ripen from the inside out—to tell whether they are ready, press gently near the stem with your thumb; it should give slightly.

Peas

Fresh peas have a very short shelf life—they lose their sweetness and become starchy soon after they are picked. There is an old joke that when cooking corn, you should put a pot of water on to boil, then rush over to the field to pick a few ears; the same applies to peas. If you can, buy them at a farm stand and cook them as soon as possible. When really fresh peas aren't available, frozen are a better alternative. Adding a tiny pinch of sugar to the cooking water can enhance the flavor of peas.

Peppers

Good raw or cooked, peppers start out green and turn red, brown, orange, or yellow as they ripen. Buy peppers with a firm, taut surface, bright green stems, and no bruises. Keep them in the refrigerator to prevent spoiling.

To seed a pepper quickly, stand it on a cutting board with the stem end up. With the blade of a large chef's knife parallel to the stem and just beyond it, cut straight down to remove one quarter of the pepper. Turn the pepper and repeat, then continue all around until the pepper is in quarters. Discard the core, stem, and seeds, which should be in one piece.

Potatoes

Italian cooks use all-purpose potatoes. I use Yukon Golds or another small waxy potato.

Look for potatoes with a smooth, clean surface. Keep them in a cool, dark, dry place; any that sprout or turn greenish should be discarded.

Stone Fruits

Apricots, plums, peaches, and nectarines are called stone fruits because of their large pits. Store them on the countertop, where they will ripen in 1 to 3 days. A slight softening along the raised "seam" of peaches and nectarines indicates ripening. Once ripe, stone fruits can be stored in the crisper drawer of the refrigerator for a few more days. They bruise easily, so handle them gently.

Tomatoes

I can be obsessive about tomatoes, because I cook with them often and like to use the best. In summer I grow some in pots on my terrace and supplement them with tomatoes from the farmers' market.

Most of the year, though, I rely on canned tomatoes. Italian peeled tomatoes from the San Marzano region are the best, because they are picked when they are tender and fully ripe. Make sure the label says "product of Italy" or "produced in Italy," or you are not getting the real thing.

Fresh tomatoes should always be kept at room temperature. Refrigerated, they become mealy and lose their flavor. Keep them stem side up on a countertop, out of the sun, and use them as soon as they are fully ripe.

Watermelons

Small yellow- and red-fleshed watermelons are a welcome sight in the summer. They are easy to carry home and store.

All watermelons, whether big or small, should have a smooth surface and feel heavy for their size. Store in the refrigerator.

Winter Squashes (Butternut, Acorn, Pumpkin, and other varieties)

With their beautiful colors, different textures, and sweet flavor, winter squashes are the stars of the fall table. Butternut is probably my favorite. Look for bright color and unblemished skin when choosing squashes. Store at room temperature or in the refrigerator.

Cutting winter squashes can be challenging, because they are so hard and unwieldy. Start by trimming off the stem end and base. Smaller squashes, such as acorn, can be cut in half and roasted, while larger squashes can be cut into pieces before peeling them. Scrape out the seeds (you can roast them to eat as a snack) and peel off the skin with a sharp vegetable peeler.

Zucchini and Other Summer Squashes

A most versatile vegetable, zucchini can be eaten raw or cooked, stuffed, stewed, fried, or in soup. Practically the whole plant is edible. Italians stuff and fry the flowers, and Sicilians cook the vines (known as *tenerumi*) and leaves in soup (see page 65).

There are many other different kinds of summer squashes, including yellow, ribbed green Romanesco, cucumber, and scallop. Buy unblemished squashes with smooth skins. Store them loosely wrapped in plastic bags in the refrigerator.

Grit can sometimes be embedded in the skin, so scrub them gently with a vegetable brush and then trim off the ends.

Antipasti

Green Olives with Spicy Bread Crumbs   14

Black-and-White Bean Spread   16

Roasted Eggplant and Pepper Spread   17

Orange Beets and Gorgonzola in Endive Leaves   18

Minted Sweet-and-Sour Eggplant   20

Parmesan-Stuffed Mushrooms   21

Stuffed Cremini Mushrooms   22

Frittatine (Mini Frittatas)   23

Roman-Style Stuffed Zucchini Flowers   24

Spinach and Cheese Fritters   26

Melted Provolone with Tomatoes and Oregano   27

Roasted Tomatoes on the Vine with Burrata or Mozzarella   28

Stuffed Artichokes   30

Roasted Peppers with Capers and Provolone   32

Farinata (Chickpea Pancake) with Green Onions   33

Truffle Parmesan Bignè (Puffs)   35

Other Appetizers

Crostini (pages 38–47)

Fried Polenta with Mushrooms (page 113)

Mascarpone or ricotta and Crostini (page 40) with Pistachio-Parsley Pesto (page 175)

Cranberry-Fig Mostarda (page 180) with goat cheese or salami

Spicy Onion Marmalade (page 179) with salami

Stuffed Eggplant Balls (page 192)

Ricotta and Tomato Crostata (page 208)

Baked Balsamic Butternut Squash (page 219)

Roasted Cauliflower with Raisins and Capers (page 226)

Utica Greens (page 251)

Green Olives with Spicy Bread Crumbs

*S*unday lunch in Rome means big family gatherings at the neighborhood trattoria. The meal often begins with an assortment of antipasti, served family-style. Roasted peppers, baked eggplant, warm slices of frittata, sautéed zucchini, fresh mozzarella, marinated anchovies, little meatballs, and pickled vegetables are among the more common offerings. I can make a whole meal of them!

One day at Sant'lgnazio, a favorite trattoria, the assortment included warm sautéed green olives with spicy bread crumbs. I loved the way cooking brought out the flavor of the mild olives, and the bread crumbs added a delicious crunch. I serve these with drinks before a meal or as part of my own antipasti tray when I have company.

Serves 8

¼ cup extra-virgin olive oil

2 tablespoons chopped fresh parsley

1 garlic clove, finely chopped

Pinch of crushed red pepper

2 cups imported green olives such as Sicilian, drained, rinsed, and patted dry

1 tablespoon red or white wine vinegar

½ cup plain dry bread crumbs

In a medium skillet over medium heat, heat the oil with the parsley, garlic, and red pepper over medium heat until fragrant. Add the olives to the pan, along with the vinegar, and cook, stirring, until the olives are warm and the vinegar has evaporated, about 3 minutes.

With a slotted spoon, transfer the olives to a serving bowl.

Add the bread crumbs to the pan and cook, stirring constantly, until evenly toasted, about 3 minutes more. Toss the olives with the bread crumbs and serve warm.

Black-and-White Bean Spread

*E*very time I go to Felidia, the classic Italian restaurant in New York City owned by the great chef Lidia Bastianich, I can't resist the luscious bean dip drizzled with black olive puree that appears on the table with the basket of bread. At Felidia, the spread is served with crackers, bread, or focaccia, but I also like it with crostini or cut-up raw vegetables.

Because I like it so much, I came up with my own version. It makes a great fast appetizer, since I always keep black olive paste and canned beans on hand (of course you can make it with cooked dried beans). Black olive paste is available in shops that specialize in Mediterranean foods and online (see Sources, page 316).

Serves 6

1 (16-ounce) can cannellini beans or 2 cups cooked beans (see page 106) with some of their liquid

1 small garlic clove

3 tablespoons extra-virgin olive oil

Salt

2 tablespoons chopped fresh parsley

Crushed red pepper

1 tablespoon black olive paste

1 recipe Crostini (Olive Oil Toasts; page 38)

If using canned beans, drain them, reserving the liquid. Place the beans, garlic, and 2 tablespoons of the oil in a food processor and blend until smooth, adding some of the liquid as needed to make a smooth paste. Add salt to taste.

Scrape the puree into a serving bowl. Sprinkle with the parsley and red pepper. Spoon the olive paste on top and swirl it in slightly for a marbleized look. Drizzle with the remaining tablespoon of oil. Serve with the crostini.

Roasted Eggplant and Pepper Spread

*C*aponata is a Sicilian vegetable mixture made with fried eggplant and other vegetables simmered in a tomato and celery sauce and seasoned with vinegar and sugar. The flavor is rich from the frying and complex from the assortment of vegetables, and it has a slightly sweet and tangy finish. In Sicily, caponata is eaten at room temperature as an antipasto, as a topping for crostini, or as a side dish.

One day I decided to season some roasted vegetables like caponata. Instead of the wine vinegar that would be used in Sicily, I used some naturally sweet balsamic vinegar, so I didn't need to add sugar. The result was this flavorful spread, not quite as complex in flavor as caponata, but satisfying nonetheless—and much easier to prepare. Exact quantities are not of great importance here, but do make sure that the vegetables are not crowded together, so that they brown nicely and take on a rich caramelized flavor.

Serve with crostini or as a side dish.

Serves 6 to 8

1 medium eggplant, trimmed and cut into 1-inch pieces

2 large red bell peppers, cut into 1-inch squares

2 medium onions, cut into 1-inch cubes

2 medium tomatoes, cut into 1-inch cubes

2 garlic cloves

⅓ cup extra-virgin olive oil

Salt

About 2 tablespoons balsamic vinegar

Preheat the oven to 425°F.

Oil a 17-x-12-x-1-inch baking sheet. Scatter the vegetables and garlic in the pan. Drizzle with the olive oil and sprinkle with salt to taste. Toss the vegetables and spread them out evenly.

Bake for 20 minutes. Stir the vegetables and bake for 15 to 20 minutes more, or until browned and tender. (You could serve the vegetables at this point as a side dish.) Let cool slightly.

Scrape the vegetables into a food processor and coarsely chop. Blend in the vinegar and season to taste with salt.

Serve immediately or cover and refrigerate for up to 3 days. Bring to room temperature before serving.

Orange Beets and Gorgonzola in Endive Leaves

This appetizer was inspired by a beautiful salad I enjoyed in Treviso, in Northern Italy. It was made with long spears of a variety of radicchio known as Tardivo and sweet red beets in an orange dressing. Since I don't often see Tardivo here, I came up with the idea of substituting crunchy boats of Belgian endive. They are convenient little containers to stuff with the salad and crumbled Gorgonzola. These are light, colorful, and easy to eat, three things I look for in an appetizer, in addition to deliciousness.

Serves 4

1 navel orange, scrubbed

2 medium beets, cooked, peeled, and cut into matchsticks (about 1 cup)

1 tablespoon extra-virgin olive oil

Salt and freshly ground pepper

2 endives, trimmed and separated into leaves

1 ounce Gorgonzola dolce, crumbled

Grate ½ teaspoon zest from the orange. Cut the orange in half and squeeze 2 tablespoons juice into a medium bowl.

Add the beets to the orange juice, along with the zest, olive oil, and salt and pepper to taste, and stir well. (*The beets can be refrigerated for up to 1 hour.*)

Just before serving, drain the beets, then scoop them into the endive leaves. Sprinkle with the Gorgonzola and serve.

Note: To cook beets, trim off the tops and stems. Wrap the beets in aluminum foil and bake at 450°F for 45 minutes, or until they are tender when pierced with a knife. Let cool, then peel off the skins.

Minted Sweet-and-Sour Eggplant

*M*int is probably the most-used herb in Sicilian kitchens. It adds a refreshing summery flavor to these fried eggplants simmered in sweet-and-sour tomato sauce.

Tomato sauce isn't the only dish where mint is used. Sicilian cooks sprinkle fresh or dried mint over salads made with potatoes, tomatoes, or green beans, use it in marinades for chicken or fish, and even add it to pesto. Though there are many types of mint, spearmint is the one most used in Sicily. It grows easily and dries well, so whether you buy more than you can use or you grow it yourself, dry some branches to add a bit of Sicilian summer sparkle to winter dishes too.

Like many Sicilian dishes, this eggplant is seasoned with vinegar and sugar, a legacy of several centuries of Arab rule. The flavors mellow as it stands, so let it rest for at least a few hours, or a day or two, in the refrigerator before serving. It is very good just with bread, or with tuna preserved in olive oil or with hard-cooked eggs.

Serves 6

Olive or vegetable oil for frying

2 medium eggplants (about 1 pound each), trimmed and cut into 1-inch cubes

2 tablespoons extra-virgin olive oil

1 medium onion, thinly sliced

⅓ cup red wine vinegar

1 tablespoon sugar

1 teaspoon salt

1 cup tomato puree

¼ cup chopped fresh mint or basil

Heat about ½ inch of the olive or vegetable oil in a large deep skillet over medium heat. Test the oil by dropping in a cube of eggplant—it should sizzle rapidly. Add enough of the eggplant to the skillet to form a single layer and cook, stirring occasionally, until nicely browned on all sides. Remove the eggplant with a slotted spoon and drain it on paper towels. Continue browning the remaining eggplant in the same way.

In a large skillet, heat the extra-virgin olive oil over medium heat. Add the onion and cook, stirring often, until tender but not browned.

Stir together the vinegar, sugar, and salt in a small bowl. Add the eggplant, tomato puree, and vinegar mixture to the skillet with the onion and cook, stirring occasionally, until slightly thickened, about 5 minutes. Stir in the mint and transfer to a medium bowl.

Let cool, then cover and refrigerate for at least several hours, or overnight. Serve at room temperature.

Parmesan-Stuffed Mushrooms

*S*tuffed mushrooms may seem like something from the 1980s, but they always disappear fast at parties. Hot and cheesy, these are just right for a passed appetizer or as part of an antipasto assortment. The tasty stuffing here is made from fresh bread crumbs, Parmigiano-Reggiano, and a bit of rosemary.

For variety, try using different cheeses or herbs in the filling. But don't stop there. You can also add prepared pesto sauce, cooked spinach, or chopped prosciutto. Small to medium mushrooms are the best choice so that they can be eaten in a bite or two.

Serves 4 to 6

12 large white or cremini mushrooms, cleaned and trimmed

1 slice Italian-style bread, torn into small bits (about ½ cup)

¼ cup whole milk

1 large egg

1 large egg yolk

1 cup freshly grated Parmigiano-Reggiano

½ teaspoon chopped fresh rosemary

Salt and freshly ground pepper

2 tablespoons extra-virgin olive oil

Preheat the oven to 350°F. Oil a baking dish large enough to hold the mushroom caps in a single layer.

Snap off the mushroom stems and chop them fine. Set the caps aside.

Soak the bread crumbs in the milk, then squeeze out the excess milk. Place the crumbs in a bowl and add the egg, egg yolk, cheese, rosemary, and salt and pepper to taste. Add the mushroom stems and mix well.

With a small spoon, scoop a little of the filling into each mushroom cap, mounding it slightly; do not press down or pack the stuffing. Place the mushrooms in the baking dish and drizzle with the oil.

Bake for 30 minutes, or until the filling is lightly browned. Serve hot.

Stuffed Cremini Mushrooms

*C*remini mushrooms, sometimes called Baby Bellas, are smaller relatives of portobellos. With a firmer texture and a bit more flavor than white mushrooms, to which they are also related, they add a little something extra to this classic preparation. The filling of dry bread crumbs flavored with garlic and cheese becomes crunchy, a nice contrast to the juicy mushroom caps.

This was one of my mom's favorite recipes, and we never failed to have them with roast beef or a steak. Look for small mushrooms that can be eaten in one or two bites.

Serves 4 to 6

1 (8- to 10-ounce) package small cremini or white mushrooms, cleaned and trimmed

½ cup plain dry bread crumbs

1 small garlic clove, minced

2 tablespoons finely chopped fresh parsley

½ cup freshly grated Pecorino Romano

Salt and freshly ground pepper

About ¼ cup extra-virgin olive oil

Preheat the oven to 375°F. Oil a baking dish large enough to hold the mushroom caps in a single layer.

Snap off the mushroom stems and chop them fine. Set the caps aside.

Place the chopped stems in a bowl and add the bread crumbs, garlic, parsley, cheese, and salt and pepper to taste. Add 2 to 3 tablespoons oil, or enough to moisten the crumbs.

Lightly stuff the mushroom caps with the filling; do not press down or pack the filling. Place the stuffed mushrooms in the baking dish and drizzle with a thin stream of oil.

Bake for 35 to 45 minutes, or until the mushrooms are tender and the crumbs are crisp and lightly browned. Serve hot or at room temperature.

Frittatine (Mini Frittatas)

*S*ilver-dollar-size frittatas flavored with tender, sweet cabbage and leeks are good served hot as an antipasto, or for breakfast, or with a salad for lunch, or tucked into rolls with sliced tomatoes for sandwiches. I first ate them in Piedmont, in Northern Italy, where they were part of an antipasti platter alongside roasted peppers, olives, and marinated mushrooms. I often make up a batch on the weekend so that I can enjoy the leftovers as a quick meal during the week when I am busy. They keep for about 3 days.

Serves 4

About ¼ cup extra-virgin olive oil

3 cups finely shredded cabbage

1 medium leek, trimmed, chopped, and well washed

6 large eggs

½ cup freshly grated Parmigiano-Reggiano

¼ teaspoon salt

Freshly ground pepper

In a large heavy skillet, heat 3 tablespoons of the olive oil over medium-low heat. Stir in the cabbage and leek, cover, and cook, stirring occasionally, until the cabbage is very tender, about 15 minutes. Let cool.

In a large bowl, whisk together the eggs, cheese, salt, and pepper to taste. Stir in the cabbage mixture.

Lightly brush a griddle or large skillet with olive oil and heat over medium heat. Stir the egg mixture and scoop by ¼-cupfuls onto the griddle, spacing the frittatas about 4 inches apart. Flatten them slightly with the back of a spoon and cook until the edges are set and the frittatas are beginning to brown on the bottom, about 2 minutes. With a pancake turner, flip the frittatas and cook for about 1 minute more, until lightly browned. Transfer the frittatas to a plate. Cook the remainder of the frittatas in the same way, brushing the griddle with more oil as needed.

Serve hot, warm, or cold.

Roman-Style Stuffed Zucchini Flowers

For this little appetizer, which is sensational with a glass of chilled Prosecco, zucchini flowers are stuffed with a bit of anchovy and mozzarella, coated in batter, and fried. The cheese and anchovy filling melts, while the batter forms a crisp shell. The combination of flour and cornstarch makes the coating particularly light and crispy.

If you are picking your own zucchini flowers, look for those that are still partially closed. Check inside the flowers, in case any insects have taken up residence.

The flavor of zucchini flowers is delicate and mildly squash-like, and they are excellent in risotto, frittatas, and fritters. The female flowers eventually produce squash, while the male flowers do not, so choose the males for cooking. You can tell which is which by looking at the stem of the flower—the males have slim green stems and the female stems resemble miniature squashes.

If you don't grow your own, squash flowers are often available at farmers' markets. The flowers are best used the same day they are harvested.

Serves 4 to 6

12 zucchini or other squash flowers

4 ounces fresh mozzarella, patted dry and cut into 1-x-½-x-½-inch strips

6 anchovy fillets, drained, halved, and patted dry

⅔ cup unbleached all-purpose flour

3 tablespoons cornstarch

½ teaspoon baking powder

¼ teaspoon salt

About ¾ cup very cold club soda or sparkling water

Peanut or vegetable oil for deep-frying

Gently wipe the flowers clean with a damp paper towel. Open the flowers and tuck a piece of mozzarella and a piece of anchovy into the center of each one. Pinch the flowers closed.

In a shallow bowl, stir together the dry ingredients. Just before using, gradually stir in enough club soda to make a mixture about as thick as pancake batter. Don't stir it too much; it's okay if there are some lumps.

Heat about 1 inch of oil in a large deep frying pan until the temperature reads 370°F on a deep-fry thermometer; a few drops of the batter added to the pan should sizzle and cook quickly.

Hold a flower by the open end to keep it from opening, dip it in the batter, turning to coat all sides, and carefully slip it into the hot oil without splashing. Add additional flowers, without crowding the pan, and fry, turning once, until crisp on both sides, about 1 minute. Remove the flowers with a slotted spoon and drain on paper towels. Repeat with the remaining flowers.

Serve hot—be sure to warn guests that the filling may be hotter than it appears!

Spinach and Cheese Fritters

$\mathcal{C}$risp on the outside and creamy within, these cheesy fritters are the kind of thing you are likely to find at one of Naples' many *friggitorie*, shops that specialize in fried foods. Neapolitans eat them as a snack or as a starter with other fried tidbits before a pizza meal. I serve them as an appetizer with drinks, salads, or other antipasti.

Makes 25 fritters

1 (10-ounce) package frozen chopped spinach, cooked and drained

8 ounces whole- or part-skim-milk ricotta

1 large egg, beaten

½ cup freshly grated Parmigiano-Reggiano

Pinch of grated lemon zest

¼ teaspoon salt

Freshly ground pepper

Pinch of freshly grated nutmeg

½ cup plain dry bread crumbs

Vegetable oil for frying

Wrap the spinach in a kitchen towel and squeeze it well to extract the excess liquid. Place the spinach on a cutting board and finely chop it.

In a bowl, whisk together the ricotta, egg, cheese, lemon zest, salt, pepper to taste, and nutmeg. Add the spinach and mix well.

Put the bread crumbs in a small shallow bowl. Scoop a heaping tablespoon of the fritter mixture into the bread crumbs, turning to coat it on all sides, then place it on a rack set over a baking sheet. Repeat with the remaining mixture. Refrigerate for 30 minutes to allow the fritters to set up.

Heat about 2 inches of oil in a medium heavy saucepan over medium-high heat until the temperature reaches 370°F on a deep-fry thermometer; a few bread crumbs dropped into the oil should sizzle immediately. Add half of the fritters and cook, turning them as needed, until lightly browned on all sides, about 4 minutes. Remove with a slotted spoon and drain on paper towels. Repeat with the remaining fritters. (*The fritters can be fried up to 3 hours ahead of serving and set aside at room temperature. Reheat in a 350°F oven before serving.*)

Serve hot.

Melted Provolone with Tomatoes and Oregano

*H*ere is a way to satisfy your pizza cravings without going to the trouble of making a pie. Melty cheese and oregano-scented tomatoes demand lots of good bread. My favorite kind is a twisted Sicilian-style semolina loaf generously sprinkled with sesame seeds. Caciocavallo, which is similar to provolone, means "horse cheese," but horses have nothing to do with it: It is made from cow's milk, and its name comes from the way the cheeses were tied together in pairs and slung over a pole to age—like saddlebags on a horse.

Serves 4 to 6

6 ounces imported Italian provolone or caciocavallo

2 tablespoons extra-virgin olive oil

1 cup halved cherry or grape tomatoes, cut in half

1 large garlic clove, minced

¼ teaspoon dried oregano

1 tablespoon red wine vinegar

Good bread for serving

Trim the rind off the cheese. Cut the cheese into ½-inch-thick slices.

In a large nonstick skillet, heat the oil over medium heat. Add the tomatoes and garlic and cook, stirring often, until the tomatoes are softened, about 3 minutes. Push the tomatoes aside and add the cheese slices in a single layer. Cook just until the cheese begins to melt, about 2 minutes; it should still hold its shape softly. Flip the slices and sprinkle with the oregano. Drizzle with the vinegar and cook for 1 minute more.

Transfer to a platter and serve hot with bread.

Roasted Tomatoes on the Vine with Burrata or Mozzarella

*E*veryone loves the combination of sweet ripe tomatoes and milky fresh cheese. Burrata is one of my favorite cheeses. It is made by shaping fresh mozzarella into a pocket and stuffing it with cream and shreds of mozzarella.

I used to make this dish only in the summer, but I've discovered that roasting can make even out-of-season tomatoes taste more tomatoey, concentrating and enhancing their flavor.

Tomatoes on the vine look pretty, but if they are not available, substitute any small tomatoes. Serve with plenty of bread to sop up the juices.

Serves 4

---

1 pound small tomatoes on the vine or cherry or grape tomatoes

¼ cup extra-virgin olive oil

Salt and freshly ground pepper

1 pound burrata or fresh mozzarella, cut into 8 slices, at room temperature

Fresh basil leaves

Italian bread for serving

Preheat the oven to 375°F.

In a baking pan just large enough to hold them, toss the tomatoes with the oil and salt and pepper to taste. Roast for 20 minutes, or until the skins are wrinkled and the tomatoes are beginning to collapse. Let cool slightly.

Arrange the cheese slices on four plates. Place the tomatoes next to the cheese. Spoon the tomato juices over all. Garnish with the basil and serve with the bread.

Stuffed Artichokes

*T*hese bread-crumb-stuffed artichokes are a far cry from the heavy, soggy versions you might have encountered. The filling is light and flavorful, just enough to season the artichokes without weighing them down.

Whenever I eat an artichoke, I think of a line from the old movie *Pat and Mike*. Spencer Tracy played Mike, a sports promoter, Katharine Hepburn played Pat, a champion golfer and all-around athlete. Singing Pat's praises, Mike says, "Not much meat on her, but what's there is 'cherce.'"

Artichokes don't have much meat on them either, but what's there is, indeed, choice. The trick is getting to it. Trimming artichokes isn't difficult, but it does take a bit of time. And they darken quickly once they are cut, so it helps to drop them into a lemon-water bath. You can use the squeezed-out lemon to lighten any artichoke stains on your hands.

Serves 6

Juice of 1 lemon

6 medium artichokes (about 8 ounces each)

½ cup plain dry bread crumbs

½ cup freshly grated Pecorino Romano or Parmigiano-Reggiano

¼ cup chopped fresh parsley

1 large garlic clove, minced

Salt and freshly ground pepper

¼ cup extra-virgin olive oil

Fill a large bowl with water and add lemon juice. With a large knife, trim off the top 1 inch of each artichoke. Cut off the stems of the artichokes. Peel off the tough outer skin of the stems with a vegetable peeler and put the stems in the bowl. Rinse the artichokes well under cold water. Working with one artichoke at a time, bend back and snap off the small leaves around the base. With kitchen shears, trim the pointed tips off the remaining leaves. To remove the choke, gently spread the artichoke leaves apart and use a small knife or a sharp spoon with a rounded tip to scrape out the fuzzy leaves in the center. Drop the artichoke into the lemon water.

Pat the stems dry. Finely chop them. In a small bowl, mix the stems with the bread crumbs, cheese, parsley, garlic, and salt and pepper to taste. Add 2 tablespoons of the olive oil to moisten the crumbs evenly.

Drain the artichokes. Holding an artichoke over the bowl of stuffing, push some of the bread crumb mixture into the center and between the leaves. Repeat with the remaining artichokes.

Place the artichokes in a pot just wide enough to hold them upright. Pour water to a depth of about ¾ inch around them and drizzle with the remaining 2 tablespoons olive oil. Cover the pot and place it over medium heat. When the water comes to a simmer, reduce the heat to low. Cook until the artichoke bottoms are tender when pierced with a knife and a leaf pulls out easily, about 45 minutes; add additional water if needed to prevent scorching.

Serve warm or at room temperature.

VARIATION

Sicilian cooks often leave out the cheese and add some chopped anchovies and capers to the bread crumb mixture.

Roasted Peppers
with Capers and Provolone

I like to pair roasted peppers with a sharp aged cheese like provolone or a mild cheese like mozzarella or ricotta salata. They are also great with anchovies as an antipasto, stuffed into sandwiches, in frittatas, or as a first course with nothing more than some good bread. The dressing for the peppers is a simple one, flavored with basil or oregano and garlic; I halve the garlic and then remove it before serving so that it doesn't overwhelm.

There are any number of ways to roast peppers. This method is my favorite, because it's much easier to remove the seeds before the peppers are cooked and you don't have to watch them constantly as you do when they are grilled or broiled.

Don't hesitate to make a big batch of these. They keep well in the refrigerator, and without the dressing, the roasted peppers can even be frozen.

Serves 4 to 6

4 large red or yellow bell peppers

1 garlic clove, halved

¼ cup chopped fresh basil or ½ teaspoon dried oregano

2 tablespoons salt-packed capers, rinsed and drained

Salt and freshly ground pepper

¼ cup extra-virgin olive oil

6 ounces imported Italian provolone, cut into thin slices

Place a rack in the top third of the oven and preheat the oven to 425°F. Line a large baking sheet with foil.

Cut around each pepper stem with a small sharp knife and remove the stem, core, and seeds. Cut the peppers in half lengthwise. Arrange cut side down on the prepared pan, flattening them with your palm.

Roast the peppers until the skin is spotted with brown and blistered, about 40 minutes, rotating the pan if necessary so that the peppers brown evenly. Remove the pan from the oven and let cool.

With your fingers, pull off and discard the pepper skin. Cut the peppers into strips and place in a bowl. Add the garlic, basil, capers, salt and pepper to taste, and the olive oil and toss well. Let stand for at least 30 minutes. (*The peppers can be made up to 24 hours ahead and refrigerated.*)

Just before serving, remove the garlic. Arrange the pepper salad in the center of a shallow serving platter, surround with the cheese, and serve.

Farinata (Chickpea Pancake) with Green Onions

*S*lices of this chickpea pancake are sold as street food in Genoa and towns all along the Riviera. The best are baked in wood-fired ovens, but an ordinary home oven and broiler also does a great job.

Instead of the scallions, you can top the farinata with fresh rosemary or sage leaves. I serve it cut into strips as an appetizer or with a green salad for dinner.

Chickpea flour is available in Italian markets, health food stores, and online.

Serves 8

1½ cups cold water

2 cups chickpea flour

2 teaspoons salt

⅓ cup extra-virgin olive oil

Coarsely ground pepper

½ cup thinly sliced scallions

Pour the water into a large bowl. Whisk the chickpea flour and salt into the water until smooth. Add the oil and whisk again. The consistency should be like a thin pancake batter. Let stand at room temperature for 1 hour.

Place an oven rack about 5 inches from the broiler and preheat the oven to 450°F. Oil a 12-x-9-x-2-inch flameproof baking pan.

Stir the batter and pour it into the prepared pan. Sprinkle with coarse pepper to taste. Bake for 5 minutes, or until the pancake begins to firm up.

Turn on the broiler and cook until the top is lightly browned, about 5 minutes more. Sprinkle with the scallions. Cut into strips and serve hot.

Truffle Parmesan Bignè (Puffs)

*A*t a wine bar in Florence, we munched on cheesy little puffs called *bignè* (pronounced *bean*-yay), flecked with black truffles, as we sipped our Prosecco. I decided to try my hand at making them by substituting black truffle butter for regular butter in my cheese puff recipe. I can't imagine a more festive party starter!

Truffles are tubers that grow underground near the roots of certain trees. So far, no one has managed to cultivate them on a large scale, and since finding them in the wild is hard work, they can be extremely expensive. Truffle butter, however, is an affordable luxury that has become more widely available. Look for it in gourmet markets or online (see Sources, page 316).

Makes about 65 puffs

1 cup water

½ teaspoon salt

4 ounces black truffle butter (see headnote)

1 cup unbleached all-purpose flour

4 large eggs

1½ cups freshly grated Parmigiano-Reggiano

Preheat the oven to 400°F. Grease two large baking sheets.

Put the water and salt in a medium heavy saucepan and bring to a boil, then stir in the butter until melted. Add the flour all at once and cook over medium heat, stirring with a wooden spoon, until the mixture pulls away from the sides of the pan. Continue to cook and stir for 1 minute more to remove excess moisture from the dough. Remove from the heat.

Add the eggs one at a time, beating well with a wooden spoon or hand-held electric mixer on high speed after each addition until incorporated. Add the cheese and beat until blended.

Scoop up a tablespoon of the mixture and use a second spoon to push it onto one of the baking sheets. Continue making small mounds of dough, placing them about 1 inch apart so that they have room to expand. Then dip your finger into cold water and pat each one to smooth the tops. (*You can make these up to 1 day ahead of time. Cover them loosely with foil and refrigerate until ready to bake.*)

Bake for 18 to 20 minutes, or until golden brown and crisp. Serve warm, or transfer the puffs to a wire rack and let cool completely.

The puffs can be stored in tightly sealed plastic bags in the refrigerator for up to 2 days or frozen for up to 1 month. Reheat them in a 350°F oven, without thawing beforehand if frozen, for about 10 minutes.

Crostini, Panini, and Pizza

Crostini (Olive Oil Toasts)

*S*lices of toasted crusty bread brushed with olive oil are the foundation of many a quick appetizer or simple meal. I keep a plastic bag of sliced bread in the freezer ready to be toasted on a moment's notice.

Be sure to use good bread for crostini. It should be a bit chewy, not cottony. White, sourdough, and whole wheat are all good.

Makes 12 crostini

12 (½-inch-thick) slices rustic bread

About 3 tablespoons extra-virgin olive oil

Place a rack in the center of the oven and preheat the oven to 375°F.

Arrange the bread in a single layer on a large baking sheet. Bake for 5 to 10 minutes, or until lightly browned and crisp. Remove from the oven.

Brush the bread on one side with the olive oil. Serve hot or at room temperature.

VARIATIONS

- For garlic toasts, rub the hot bread with a garlic clove, then brush with the oil.

- Add a pinch of dried oregano or thyme and a sprinkle of salt and pepper to the olive oil before brushing the toasts.

- Substitute melted butter for the oil.

Herbed Goat Cheese–Ricotta Crostini

*W*hipped together, ricotta and fresh goat cheese become smooth and creamy. Topped with herbs and extra-virgin olive oil, the blend makes a tempting spread for crostini. In Sicily, the crostini would be made with just sheep's-milk ricotta, which has an herbal flavor that is similar to a mild goat cheese. Unfortunately, it isn't easy to find here. The late Anna Tasca Lanza, who ran a cooking school at Regaleali, her family's Sicilian winery, suggested this substitute to me.

Serves 6

1 (15-ounce) container whole-milk ricotta

1 (5-ounce) log soft fresh goat cheese

1 teaspoon fresh marjoram leaves

1 teaspoon fresh thyme leaves

1 teaspoon chopped fresh chives

½ teaspoon kosher salt or coarse sea salt

1 teaspoon coarsely cracked pepper

3 tablespoons extra-virgin olive oil

1 recipe Crostini (opposite)

Combine the ricotta and goat cheese in a food processor and process until smooth. Spread the cheese on a small serving plate.

Sprinkle with the herbs, salt, and pepper, drizzle with the olive oil, and serve with the crostini.

Breakfast Crostini

$\mathcal{C}$rostini are delightful for breakfast too. Spread warm toasted bread with a soft creamy cheese like mascarpone or ricotta, add some sliced fresh figs or another fruit in season, drizzle with good honey, and finish with a sprinkling of sliced almonds. Serve them with a fresh fruit salad and a pot of caffè latte, preferably on a sunny terrace, for an Italian-inspired start to the day.

Italian chestnut honey is delicious: The flavor is slightly smoky, spicy, and more aromatic than that of other honeys. In Tuscany they eat it drizzled over aged Pecorino cheese, while in Piedmont they serve it with Gorgonzola and walnuts.

Serves 4 to 6

1 recipe Crostini (page 38), still warm

1 cup (8 ounces) mascarpone or ricotta cheese

12 ripe figs, thickly sliced

2 tablespoons Italian chestnut honey or other aromatic honey

2 tablespoons sliced almonds (with skins), toasted

Spread the crostini with the mascarpone. Arrange the fig slices on top. Drizzle with the honey, sprinkle with the almonds, and serve.

Avocado and Bottarga Crostini

Bottarga, sometimes called Mediterranean caviar, is cured pressed fish roe. It comes from Sardinia and Sicily and is also eaten in other parts of the Mediterranean. The flavor is briny and, yes, a bit fishy—but in a good way! Italians like to shave thin slices and toss it with spaghetti or salad, or simply serve it on top of crostini.

Bottarga goes beautifully with mild, buttery, and soft ingredients. The sight of a ripe avocado on my kitchen counter provided one of those great culinary aha! moments. I put the two together on some crostini, sprinkled them with coarsely ground black pepper, and drizzled on some olive oil. (The bottarga supplied all the salt needed.) Now this is my favorite way to eat both avocados and bottarga.

Bottarga can often be found at shops that sell smoked salmon and caviar, or you can mail-order it (see Sources, page 316). Or, if you don't have bottarga, top the avocado on each crostini with a bit of anchovy, a dab of olive paste, or a sliver of sharp Pecorino cheese.

Serves 4 to 6

1 ripe Hass avocado, peeled, pitted, and thinly sliced

1 recipe Crostini (page 38)

A chunk of bottarga for shaving

Freshly ground black pepper

Extra-virgin olive oil

Coarsely mash the avocado. Spread it on the crostini.

With a swivel-blade vegetable peeler or a sharp paring knife, shave off thin slices of bottarga; you want about 1 ounce. Place the bottarga on top of the avocado, sprinkle with pepper and a few drops of oil, and serve.

Radicchio and Gorgonzola Crostini

*T*he beautiful burgundy color of radicchio darkens when it is cooked, and here it melts down and becomes tender as it marries with the sweet flavor of the raisins. A bit of balsamic vinegar adds a tangy accent, while crumbled Gorgonzola contributes a sharp and salty contrast.

Serves 6

1 head radicchio (about 8 ounces)

2 tablespoons extra-virgin olive oil

2 tablespoons raisins

¼ cup water

1 teaspoon balsamic vinegar, or to taste

Salt and freshly ground pepper

1 recipe Crostini (page 38)

2 ounces Gorgonzola dolce, crumbled

Cut the radicchio in half and remove the core. Slice each half crosswise into thin shreds.

In a large skillet, heat the oil over medium heat. Add the radicchio, raisins, and water, cover, and cook for 15 minutes, or until the radicchio is tender. Uncover and cook until the water is evaporated. Stir in the vinegar and salt and pepper to taste.

Spoon the radicchio and raisins onto the crostini. Sprinkle with the cheese and serve.

Chickpea, Sun-Dried Tomato, and Arugula Crostini

*L*ooking for a light meal in Florence, I stopped at Caffè Coquinarius, an *enoteca*, or "wine bar," practically in the shadow of the city's magnificent cathedral. With whitewashed walls and rustic wood furnishings, the restaurant was friendly and busy. It had a menu of interesting salads, an extensive selection of crostini, and a good list of local wines. I ordered the vegetarian assortment, which included toasted slices of the crusty unsalted bread for which Tuscans are famous, spread with garlicky mashed chickpeas with sweet bits of dried tomato and leaves of piquant arugula on top. With a glass of chilled white Vermentino, it was just the kind of casual meal I was looking for. Now when I want a quick lunch or speedy antipasto, I make these crostini at home.

Serves 4

¼ cup extra-virgin olive oil

1 garlic clove, finely chopped

2 tablespoons chopped fresh parsley

Pinch of crushed red pepper

1 (15-ounce) can chickpeas with their liquid

¼ cup sun-dried tomatoes (not oil-packed), chopped

Salt and freshly ground pepper

1 recipe Crostini (page 38)

Small bunch of arugula

In a medium saucepan over medium heat, heat the olive oil, garlic, parsley, and red pepper for 2 minutes, or until fragrant. Add the chickpeas, with their liquid, and the sun-dried tomatoes and cook, coarsely mashing the chickpeas with a potato masher and stirring, for 10 minutes, or until the mixture is thick and spreadable. Season with salt and pepper.

Spread the crostini with the chickpea mixture. Top with the arugula and serve.

More Toppings for Crostini

Roasted Eggplant and Pepper Spread (page 17)

Roasted Peppers with Capers and Provolone (page 32)

Uncooked Tomato Sauce (page 170)

Tiny-Tomato Sauce (page 172)

Two-Tomato Sauce (page 172)

Winter Pesto (page 174)

Pistachio-Parsley Pesto (page 175)

Walnut-Parsley Pesto (page 176)

Spicy Onion Marmalade (page 179)

Spicy Vegetable Stew (page 193)

Spinach (or Other Greens) with Garlic and Hot Pepper (page 247)

Swiss Chard with Tomato and Garlic (page 248)

Utica Greens (page 251)

Eggplant and Roasted Pepper Panini with Caper Mayonnaise

*A*toasted panino is so much more satisfying than an ordinary sandwich. With a luscious caper mayonnaise to tie together the flavors of the grilled eggplant, roasted peppers, and cheese, this one is delicious enough to serve as an appetizer, cut into bite-size pieces and speared with toothpicks, with wine or drinks.

The caper mayonnaise is good spooned over many other foods as well, such as hard-cooked eggs, sliced tomatoes, canned tuna, and green beans.

Serves 2

Caper Mayonnaise

2 tablespoons capers, rinsed and drained

½ teaspoon grated (on a Microplane) or minced garlic

3 tablespoons mayonnaise

1 tablespoon extra-virgin olive oil

4 slices sourdough, ciabatta, or other rustic bread

2 tablespoons extra-virgin olive oil

3 ounces imported Italian provolone or Asiago, thinly sliced

1 small eggplant, grilled (see page 246)

1 roasted red pepper (see page 32), cut into thin strips

To make the caper mayonnaise

Stir together the capers, garlic, mayonnaise, and olive oil until blended.

Brush one side of each bread slice with the olive oil. Spread the caper mayonnaise on the opposite side of each slice. Place half of the cheese on top of the mayonnaise on 2 slices, then top with the eggplant, roasted pepper, and remaining cheese. Close the sandwiches (oiled sides out), pressing down firmly.

Heat a stovetop grill or heavy skillet over medium heat. Add the sandwiches, weight them down with a large pot or its lid, and cook until they are toasted on the bottom, about 4 minutes. Turn the sandwiches over and cook for 3 minutes, or until the cheese is melted and the sandwiches are toasted on both sides.

Cut the panini in half and serve hot.

Zucchini Panini

I love saying "zucchini panini," and I also love to eat them. The warm cheese oozes from the crisp toasty bread, the zucchini lightens the flavor, and the olive paste adds a salty contrast. Serve this hearty sandwich with a bowl of Swiss Chard and Tomato Soup with Poached Eggs (page 68) for a delicious Sunday supper.

Serves 2

4 slices ciabatta or other chewy rustic bread, split

2 tablespoons extra-virgin olive oil

2 tablespoons black olive paste or pesto

4 ounces Asiago, imported Italian provolone, or Fontina Valle d'Aosta, sliced, (see headnote, page 54)

1 medium zucchini, grilled (see page 246)

Brush one side of each slice of bread with the oil. Spread the opposite side of 2 slices with the olive paste. Place the cheese on top of the olive paste. Add the zucchini and close the sandwiches (oiled sides out), pressing down firmly.

Heat a ridged grill pan or heavy skillet over medium heat. Add the sandwiches, weight them down with a heavy pot or its lid, and cook until they are toasted on the bottom, about 4 minutes. Turn the sandwiches over and cook for 3 minutes, or until the cheese is melted and the sandwiches are toasted on both sides.

Cut the panini in half and serve hot.

Mushroom, Arugula, and Robiola Panini

*N*utty arugula cuts the richness of the sautéed mushrooms and creamy Robiola cheese in this irresistible panino.

Robiola is a soft young cheese that is made from cow's milk or a combination of cow's, sheep's, and goat's milk. It has an edible rind and a delicious mushroomy flavor. If you can't find it, you can substitute Taleggio or fresh goat cheese.

Serves 2

¼ cup extra-virgin olive oil

8 ounces white mushrooms, cleaned, trimmed, and sliced

1 large garlic clove, halved

Salt

4 slices peasant bread or ciabatta

3 ounces Robiola, Taleggio, or soft fresh goat cheese, softened

2 cups coarsely chopped arugula

In a large skillet, heat 2 tablespoons of the oil over medium heat. Add the mushrooms and garlic, sprinkle with salt, and cook, stirring frequently, until the liquid the mushrooms release evaporates and they are tender and browned, about 10 minutes. Remove from the heat and discard the garlic.

Brush one side of each bread slice with the remaining 2 tablespoons oil. Spread the cheese on the opposite sides. Pile the mushrooms and arugula on top of the cheese. Close the sandwiches (oiled side out), pressing down firmly.

Heat a stovetop grill or heavy skillet over medium heat. Add the sandwiches, weight them down with a large pot or its lid, and cook until browned on the bottom, about 4 minutes. Turn the sandwiches over and cook on the other side for 3 minutes, or until the cheese is melted and the sandwiches are toasted on both sides.

Cut the panini in half and serve hot.

Pizza Dough

*A*revolution occurred in pizza when baker Jim Lahey, who had studied bread making in Rome, introduced his no-knead-dough technique. I was skeptical until I spoke to a friend who is a *pizzaiolo*—a professional pizza maker—who assured me the idea was sound. I was astounded to discover that instead of all that kneading, I could make dough by simply stirring together the ingredients. The results were better than any homemade pizza I had ever eaten.

The secret to this dough, which I've adapted from Lahey's method, is to handle it as gently as possible and give it a long rest—from 12 hours to 3 days—so that it can develop flavor and tenderness. Since I don't always make two pizzas at one time, I often leave the second half of the dough in the refrigerator to use later in the week. Don't roll this dough with a rolling pin; just pat it out with your fingertips so you won't lose the bubbles that have formed, and the crust will be light and crisp.

I like to use my heavy-duty mixer to mix the ingredients together, but it is easy enough to use a bowl and a wooden spoon.

Note that you'll need to make the dough the night before you plan to use it.

Makes enough for two 12-inch pizzas, one 12-inch double-crust stuffed pizza, or one 17-x-10-inch pizza

---

4 cups unbleached all-purpose flour, plus more for shaping the dough

¼ teaspoon active dry yeast

2½ teaspoons salt

1⅔ cups water

To make the dough

In the bowl of a heavy-duty mixer fitted with the dough hook, or in a large bowl with a wooden spoon, stir together the flour, yeast, and salt. On low speed, gradually add the water, mixing just until the dough forms a shaggy-looking ball, about 3 minutes. Or gradually stir in the water. Do not overwork the dough. If you used a mixer, turn the dough out into another bowl. Cover the dough with plastic wrap and leave it at cool room temperature for 12 to 18 hours (depending on the temperature), until doubled in size. Small bubbles will appear on the surface. (*Once the dough is ready, you can store it in the refrigerator for up to 3 days, until you are ready to bake it.*)

About 1 hour before you are ready to bake, turn the dough out onto a lightly floured surface. Stretch and pat the dough into a rectangle, handling it gently to avoid squeezing out the air bubbles. If making two 12-inch pizzas or a stuffed pizza, cut the dough in half. Pull the edges of the dough under and pinch them together to form a ball (or

2 balls). Place seam side down on a lightly floured board. Dust the top with flour and cover lightly with plastic wrap. Let rest for 1 hour.

Meanwhile, preheat the oven and pizza stone

About 1 hour before baking, arrange an oven rack in the upper third of the oven if using a pizza stone or in the middle of the oven if using a baking sheet. Place the stone on the rack. (Do not preheat the baking sheet.) Turn the oven to the highest temperature, 500°F to 550°F, and preheat for 1 hour.

Once the oven is fully preheated, switch on the broiler. (Note that the broiler, if it is in the oven that has been preheated, may take several minutes to come on.) Let the broiler heat for 10 minutes.

Add the toppings and bake according to the individual recipes.

VARIATION

For Whole Wheat Pizza Dough, substitute 1½ cups whole wheat flour for 1½ cups of the unbleached all-purpose flour.

Mushroom, Fontina, and Taleggio Pizza

*T*his pizza, with garlicky sautéed mushrooms, creamy Taleggio cheese, and buttery, earthy Fontina, was inspired by one I ate in Piedmont. Many cheeses are sold as Fontina, but the one to buy is Fontina Valle d'Aosta, a semi-firm cow's-milk cheese from Northern Italy. It is flavorful without being sharp and has a distinctive mushroomy aroma.

Taleggio, another cow's-milk cheese from Northern Italy, has a soft creamy texture and a pungent aroma, yet the flavor is mild and nutty. It melts beautifully, so it is perfect for a pizza topping. If you can't find Taleggio, substitute Robiola, if you can get it, or just increase the amount of Fontina.

Makes one 12-inch pizza

½ recipe Pizza Dough
(page 52)

3 ounces Fontina Valle d'Aosta
(see headnote), thinly sliced

2 ounces Taleggio cheese,
cut into small pieces

1 recipe Sautéed Mushrooms
with Garlic and Parsley
(page 238)

Preheat the oven as described on page 53.

Generously dust a pizza peel or rimless baking sheet with flour on a floured surface. Gently pat and stretch the dough out to a 12-inch circle. Don't worry if the dough is not perfectly round. Place the dough on the peel or baking sheet. Shake the peel gently. If the dough is sticking, lift it and dust with more flour.

Arrange the cheeses over the dough, leaving a 1-inch border all around. Top the cheese with the mushrooms.

If using a pizza stone, slide the pizza onto the stone and broil until the bottom of the crust is crisp and the top is blistered, 4 to 6 minutes; watch carefully so that it does not burn. *If using a baking sheet*, place the pan in the oven and bake until the bottom of the crust is browned and the top is bubbly, 6 to 8 minutes. Remember that each oven and broiler is a little different, so watch carefully to ensure a crisp brown crust without burning.

Remove the pizza from the oven and slide it onto a cutting board. Cut into wedges and serve.

Stuffed Pizza with Escarole, Olives, and Provolone

*C*hristmas Eve at our house wouldn't be the same without *pizza di scarola,* as this stuffed Neapolitan pie is called. My mother's version was filled with escarole, anchovies, and olives and seasoned with a pinch of crushed red pepper. She used homemade lard to make the crust and rather than baking the pie in the oven, she would fry it on the stovetop in a big black iron skillet, flipping it once to brown it on the second side. It always amazed me how adeptly she handled the heavy skillet filled with the sizzling hot pie. We loved the result, but the rich, oily crust made it very heavy.

Like similar pies in Naples today, my version is made with pizza dough and baked in the oven, so it is a lot easier to handle and not as rich. As a variation, I have added imported Italian provolone for a smoky cheese flavor and left out the anchovies, but both ways are traditional.

Makes one 12-inch double-crust pizza

---

1 recipe Pizza Dough (page 52), shaped into 2 balls

1½ pounds escarole, trimmed, washed, and coarsely chopped

Salt

¼ cup extra-virgin olive oil

3 large garlic cloves, thinly sliced

½ cup chopped pitted imported black olives

4 ounces imported Italian provolone, thinly sliced

While the dough is rising, make the filling: Bring about 2 inches of water to a boil in a large saucepan. Add the escarole and salt to taste and cook for 10 minutes, or until the escarole is tender. Drain the escarole in a colander and press out the excess liquid.

Dry the saucepan, add the oil and garlic, and cook over medium heat for 1 minute, or until the garlic is lightly golden. Stir in the olives, add the escarole, and toss well. Cook until any liquid evaporates. Remove from the heat and let cool.

Place a rack in the center of the oven and preheat the oven to 450°F. Oil a 12-inch pizza pan.

With your fingertips, pat and stretch one piece of dough out into a 12-inch circle on a floured surface and place it on the pan.

Spread the escarole mixture over the dough, leaving a 1-inch border all around. Arrange the cheese over the greens.

Pat out the second piece of dough and arrange it over the filling. Press the edges together firmly to seal. Fold and crimp the edges together at

1-inch intervals to form a braided border. Cut several small slits in the surface of the dough to allow steam to escape.

Bake the pizza for 35 to 40 minutes, or until the crust is golden brown and crisp. Remove from the oven and let cool for 10 minutes.

Slide the pizza onto a cutting board, cut into wedges, and serve.

Aunt Millie's Pan Pizza

*M*y Aunt Millie was famous in our family for her pizza. She baked the pies in big battered pans slicked with plenty of olive oil. The crusts were thick but very light, and the bottoms were crunchy and brown from the oil. She was freewheeling with the toppings and would use whatever she happened to have on hand, such as meatballs, anchovies, or cooked vegetables like cauliflower or broccoli. No matter what the topping, her pizza always tasted great.

Serves 8

Extra-virgin olive oil

1 recipe Pizza Dough
(page 52)

1 recipe Marinara Sauce
(page 171)

1 teaspoon dried oregano

8–12 ounces fresh mozzarella,
thinly sliced

¼ cup freshly grated Pecorino
Romano or Parmigiano-
Reggiano

2 tablespoons extra-virgin
olive oil

Preheat the oven to 450°F. Generously oil a 17-x-12-x-1-inch baking sheet. Place the dough on the pan and stretch and pat it out to fit. With your fingertips, firmly press the dough to make dimples all over the surface. Stir together the sauce and oregano. Spread the sauce over the dough, leaving a 1-inch border. Bake for 20 minutes.

Remove the pizza from the oven and arrange the cheese slices over the top. Sprinkle with the grated cheese. Drizzle with the olive oil. Return the pizza to the oven and bake for 5 minutes, or until the cheese is melted and the crust is browned.

Cut the pizza into squares and serve hot.

Soups

Cold Cucumber Cream with Tomato Salsa

One summer in Rome, the temperature hovered in the high 90s for days. We didn't have our usual appetite for classic Roman dishes, but we lapped up every bit of this cold refreshing cucumber soup topped with a colorful spoonful of tomato and basil salsa.

Serves 4

1¼ pounds cucumbers
(3–4 large or 8–10 Kirbys)

2 scallions

¾ cup water

About 1 teaspoon white wine vinegar

Salt and freshly ground pepper

1 medium tomato

1 tablespoon shredded fresh basil

1 tablespoon extra-virgin olive oil

Peel the cucumbers and cut lengthwise in half. With a small spoon, scoop out the seeds and discard them.

Finely chop enough of the cucumbers to make ½ cup. Cover and refrigerate for the salsa.

Cut the remaining cucumbers into 1-inch chunks. Chop 1 of the scallions. In a blender or food processor, combine the cucumber chunks, the chopped scallion, and the water and puree until smooth. Season to taste with the vinegar, salt, and pepper. Pour the soup into a covered container and refrigerate until cold, about 2 hours.

Just before serving, cut the tomato in half through the stem end. Remove the core and squeeze the halves to extract some of the seeds and juice; discard them. Cut the tomato into ½-inch dice and place in a small bowl. Finely chop the remaining scallion and add it to the bowl, along with the reserved chopped cucumber and the basil. Toss with the oil and salt and pepper to taste.

Taste the soup for seasoning. Spoon it into chilled bowls, top each bowl with some of the salsa, and serve.

Pugliese-Style Zucchini-Potato Soup

Cucina povera means "the cooking of the poor," but it's really all about how good Italian cooks are at making something wonderful out of very little. Two basic vegetables, a handful of pasta, and a bit of cheese are all it takes to create this hearty and warming soup. The recipe comes from the region of Puglia, the heel of the Italian boot, which is known for its creative vegetable cooking.

Italian cooks never break spaghetti unless they are using it in soup. To keep the pieces from flying around the kitchen, wrap the pasta in a kitchen towel, then break it with your hands or bash it with a small pot into spoon-size pieces. It's a perfect way to finish up a small amount of pasta left in the box. Need I mention that kids love to help with this job?

Serves 4

8 cups water

1 garlic clove, minced

1½ teaspoons salt

3 medium waxy potatoes, such as Yukon Golds, peeled and cut into ½-inch pieces

3 medium zucchini, scrubbed, trimmed, and cut into ½-inch pieces

4 ounces spaghetti, broken into small pieces (about 1 cup)

3 tablespoons extra-virgin olive oil, plus more for serving

Freshly ground pepper

½ cup freshly grated Parmigiano-Reggiano

Bring the water to a boil in a large pot. Add the garlic, salt, and potatoes and cook until the potatoes are tender, about 10 minutes.

Add the zucchini and spaghetti and cook until the spaghetti is al dente, about 10 minutes.

Stir in the oil and pepper to taste. Stir in the cheese and serve drizzled with additional oil.

Tenerumi Soup
(Squash Vine and Spaghetti Soup)

Fresh sheep's-milk ricotta still warm from the dairy, artichokes so tender you can eat them raw, and *tenerumi* cooked into a soup—a Sicilian friend was listing the foods he missed the most in America. I couldn't help him with the first two, but, I told him, I had just seen *tenerumi* in the farmers' market.

Tenerumi (also spelled *tinirumi*) are the leaves, buds, and vines of cucuzza, a pale green squash that can grow up to six feet long. The plants produce an abundance of vines, which are a nice addition to a simple soup that Sicilians make in the late summer. My friend gave me his recipe, and when I prepared it, my husband, who is 100-percent Sicilian, loved it.

Look for *tenerumi* at produce stores in Italian neighborhoods, or grow cucuzza yourself. Spinach or dandelion greens are also good.

Serves 4 to 6

6 cups water

1 large bunch tender vines with leaves (*tenerumi*) from cucuzza or zucchini (about 1 pound)

1 medium onion, finely chopped

¼ cup extra-virgin olive oil

2 garlic cloves, finely chopped

2 cups seeded and coarsely chopped tomatoes

Salt and freshly ground pepper

4 ounces spaghetti, broken into 1-inch pieces (about 1 cup)

6 large fresh basil leaves, shredded

½ cup freshly grated Pecorino Romano for serving

Bring the water to a boil in a large pot.

Meanwhile, discard the tough squash vines and wash the leaves and tender vines. Chop into bite-size pieces.

In a large skillet, cook the onion in the olive oil over medium heat until tender and golden, about 8 minutes. Stir in the garlic, tomatoes, and salt and pepper to taste and cook for 10 minutes, or until the tomato juices have thickened.

Add the greens and salt to taste to the boiling water, reduce the heat to low, and cook for 10 to 15 minutes, or until the greens are tender.

Stir the tomato sauce and pasta into the pot with the greens and cook for about 10 minutes, stirring frequently, until the pasta is tender. If the soup is too thick, stir in a little more water. Stir in the basil.

Serve hot or at room temperature, sprinkled with the cheese.

Acquacotta
(Tomato and Bread Soup)

*A*cquacotta, or "cooked water," the traditional name for this soup, suggests that not much is required to make it. It was originally a peasant dish, made with stale bread and a few tomatoes or whatever vegetables a cook had on hand, perhaps mushrooms, zucchini, or green beans. But top it with a poached egg and a sprinkling of good Tuscan Pecorino, and you have a one-dish meal fit for kings, peasants, and anyone else with good taste.

Serves 4

1 large onion, finely chopped

1 celery rib, finely chopped

3 tablespoons extra-virgin olive oil

2 garlic cloves, finely chopped

1 pound ripe plum tomatoes, chopped, with their juice, or 2 cups chopped canned Italian tomatoes, with their juice

4 cups Rich Vegetable Broth (page 88) or water

Salt and freshly ground pepper

4 large eggs

4 slices Italian bread, toasted

¼ cup freshly grated Pecorino Toscano or Parmigiano-Reggiano

4 large fresh basil leaves, torn into bits

In a large pot, cook the onion and celery in the oil over medium heat, stirring occasionally, until tender and golden, about 10 minutes. Stir in the garlic and cook for 1 minute. Add the tomatoes, with their juice, and cook, stirring occasionally, for 10 minutes.

Add the broth and salt and pepper to taste, bring to a simmer, and cook for 20 minutes.

Break 1 of the eggs into a cup and carefully slip it into the simmering soup. Repeat with the remaining eggs. Cover and cook over very low heat until the eggs are just set, about 3 minutes.

Place the bread slices in four soup bowls. Sprinkle each slice with some cheese and basil and carefully spoon an egg on top. Ladle the soup around the egg and serve.

Swiss Chard and Tomato Soup
with Poached Eggs

*S*wiss chard is at its best in early fall when the weather turns cool. For this soup, chard is cooked with tomatoes, garlic, and onion. A poached egg and a slice of toasted bread top each serving, making it a complete meal.

My favorite bread for topping soup is ciabatta because it is crisp outside and moist within, has a light, airy texture, and toasts nicely. If you can't find ciabatta, substitute another light, crispy bread.

Serves 4

1 medium onion, chopped

¼ cup extra-virgin olive oil, plus more for drizzling

3 garlic cloves, finely chopped, plus 1 whole clove

1 large fresh tomato, chopped, or 1 cup chopped canned Italian tomatoes with their juice

1½ pounds Swiss chard, trimmed and torn into bite-size pieces

1 cup water

Salt and freshly ground pepper

4 slices ciabatta, toasted

4 large eggs

½ cup freshly grated Pecorino Romano

In a large pot, cook the onion in the olive oil over medium heat for 8 minutes, or until tender and golden. Stir in the chopped garlic and tomato and cook for 5 minutes, until the tomato juices have thickened.

Add the Swiss chard to the pot, along with the water and salt and pepper to taste, cover, and cook for 10 minutes, or until the chard is tender.

Meanwhile, rub each slice of toast with the whole garlic clove. Place a slice in each of four serving bowls.

About 5 minutes before the soup is ready, bring a wide saucepan of water to a simmer and add salt to taste. Break 1 of the eggs into a small cup, carefully slip it into the water, and stir gently so that it doesn't stick to the bottom. Repeat with the remaining eggs. Cover and cook until the eggs are done to taste, about 3 minutes. With a slotted spoon, remove the eggs from the water one at a time, drain well, and place 1 egg on each slice of toast.

Ladle the soup around the toast. Sprinkle with the cheese, drizzle with a little olive oil, and serve.

Ribollita (Tuscan Bread and Vegetable Soup)

*T*uscans favor soup over pasta as a first course, and no soup is more revered in the region than this hearty vegetable one thickened with bread. I was served a version of it—each a little different from the last—just about everywhere I went when I visited Italy one September. The only common ingredients were cabbage, beans, and bread. Some cooks insisted that seven vegetables were needed; others said it didn't matter. Some soups were made with a ham bone or sautéed pancetta, while others used homemade broth or even just water. This is how I like ribollita. The soup becomes thick as it stands and is often served at room temperature.

Serves 8

2 medium onions, chopped

2 carrots, peeled and chopped

1 celery rib, chopped

1 tablespoon chopped fresh rosemary

1 teaspoon chopped fresh thyme

1 teaspoon chopped fresh sage

¼ cup extra-virgin olive oil, plus more for drizzling

½ small cabbage, cored and shredded

12 ounces kale, preferably Tuscan kale, cut into narrow strips

1 cup chopped fresh or canned Italian tomatoes

Salt

3 cups Rich Vegetable Broth (page 88) or chicken broth

3 cups water

3 cups cooked cannellini beans (see page 106) or canned beans, with their liquid

Freshly ground pepper

8 slices day-old rustic Italian bread

In a large pot, cook the onions, carrots, celery, and herbs in the oil over medium heat, stirring frequently, until the onions are golden, about 10 minutes. Add the cabbage, kale, and tomatoes and stir well. Add 1 teaspoon salt, the broth, and water, bring to a simmer, and cook for 30 minutes.

To thicken the soup, mash half the beans with a potato masher or a wire whisk and add all the beans to the pot. If necessary, add more water to just cover the vegetables. Cook for 1 hour more. Season to taste with salt and pepper. (*The soup can be made up to 3 days ahead. Let cool, then cover and refrigerate; reheat gently.*)

Place a few slices of bread in the bottom of a large serving bowl or soup tureen. Add a layer of the soup. Repeat the layering, ending with the bread. Let stand for 10 minutes, until the liquid is absorbed. Serve hot or at room temperature, drizzled with olive oil.

Broccoli, Garlic, and Pasta Soup

*B*roccoli stems make good eating, but most recipes tell you to discard them. One of the reasons I like this soup is that it uses the stems.

They are peeled to get rid of the tough skin, then simmered in a garlicky broth and pureed to make a tasty base before the pasta and delicate broccoli florets are added. You can make the base for the soup in advance and reheat it just before serving. A sprinkle of fresh parsley and a swirl of Parmigiano round out the flavors.

Serves 4

1 medium bunch broccoli (about 1¼ pounds)

3 garlic cloves, finely chopped

3 tablespoons extra-virgin olive oil

6 cups water

Salt

1 cup elbow, ditalini, or other short pasta

2 tablespoons chopped fresh parsley

Freshly ground pepper

½ cup freshly grated Parmigiano-Reggiano

Remove the broccoli florets from the stems and cut them into small bite-size pieces. Set aside. Trim the base of the stems. Peel the stems with a vegetable peeler or sharp paring knife. Cut crosswise into ½-inch-thick slices.

In a large pot, cook the garlic in the oil over medium heat until golden, about 1 minute. Add the broccoli stems, water, and salt to taste, bring to a simmer, and cook until the stems are very tender, about 30 minutes.

With a slotted spoon, transfer the stems to a food processor or blender. Process until smooth. Return the puree to the pot. (*The soup can be made ahead to this point. Let cool, cover and then refrigerate for up to 24 hours.*)

Reheat the soup until simmering. Add the pasta and broccoli florets and cook, stirring often, until the pasta is tender, about 10 minutes. Stir in the parsley, a generous grinding of pepper, and ¼ cup of the cheese. Taste for seasoning.

Serve sprinkled with the remaining ¼ cup cheese.

Broccoli Rabe and Cannellini Bean Soup

*N*eapolitans are crazy for *friarielli*, a vegetable similar in taste and appearance to broccoli rabe. They toss it with pasta, bake it on pizza with fresh or smoked mozzarella, and sauté it with garlic and hot pepper to go with sausages.

One day, after a long morning visiting Naples' famous National Archaeological Museum, which is full of stunning treasures from the ancient towns of Pompeii and Herculaneum, we stopped at a trattoria in nearby Piazza Dante for lunch. It seemed as though we were barely seated before the waiter began bringing out a series of mouthwatering vegetable antipasti. We told him we could not eat much more, but he ignored us and brought us each a bowl of soup that I have never forgotten. It was the chef's version of pasta and bean soup, a creamy, flavorful bean puree, chunky with bits of bitter *friarielli*, and pasta. This is my version, made with broccoli rabe. It's hearty and great for a winter day.

Serves 4

1 large onion, chopped

¼ cup extra-virgin olive oil

1 large garlic clove, very finely chopped

3 cups water

2 cups cooked cannellini beans (see page 106) or drained canned beans

1 cup chopped fresh or canned Italian tomatoes

Salt and freshly ground pepper

1 pound broccoli rabe, trimmed and chopped into ½-inch pieces

4 ounces broken spaghetti or small pasta shapes, such as tubetti or ditalini (about 1 cup)

In a large pot, cook the onion in the oil over medium heat until tender and golden, about 10 minutes. Stir in the garlic and cook for 1 minute. Add the water, beans, tomatoes, and salt and pepper to taste, bring to a simmer, and cook for 20 minutes, or until the tomatoes are soft.

Stir the broccoli rabe and pasta into the soup and cook, stirring frequently to prevent sticking and adding more water if the soup becomes too thick, for 20 to 30 minutes, until the greens and pasta are tender.

Taste for seasoning and serve.

Chickpea Minestrone with Broken Spaghetti

A minestra is a soup containing rice or pasta with vegetables or beans cooked in broth or water. With the flick of a suffix, the name changes to *minestrina* or *minestrella*, a light, clear version, while a *minestrone* is thick.

This hearty minestrone is one I adapted from a recipe leaflet distributed by a Tuscan winemaker. I liked the fact that the recipe contains sage and fennel, which add a lot of flavor. Tuscans serve it at room temperature with a drizzle of extra-virgin olive oil, but I like it hot with freshly grated cheese.

Serves 6

1 large onion, coarsely chopped

1 medium carrot, peeled and coarsely chopped

1 celery rib, coarsely chopped

1 small fennel bulb, trimmed and coarsely chopped

1 garlic clove, finely chopped

1 tablespoon finely chopped fresh sage or 1 teaspoon crumbled dried

3 tablespoons extra-virgin olive oil

2 tablespoons tomato paste

2 cups cooked chickpeas (see page 106) or drained canned chickpeas

3 cups Rich Vegetable Broth (page 88) or chicken broth

3 cups water

Salt and freshly ground pepper

4 ounces broken spaghetti or small pasta, such as tubetti or tiny shells (about 1 cup)

½ cup freshly grated Pecorino Romano or Parmigiano-Reggiano for serving

In a large pot, cook the onion, carrot, celery, fennel, garlic, and sage in the olive oil, stirring occasionally, until the vegetables are tender and golden, about 10 minutes. Stir in the tomato paste and cook for 2 minutes. Add the chickpeas, broth, and water, bring to a simmer, and cook for 1 hour, or until the vegetables are very tender.

Mash some of the chickpeas with the back of a spoon to thicken the soup. Season with salt and pepper to taste.

When the soup is almost ready, add the pasta and stir well. Cook, stirring occasionally, until the pasta is tender. If the soup is too thick, stir in a little warm water. Taste for seasoning.

Serve sprinkled with the cheese.

Spinach and Polenta Soup

*P*arts of Friuli-Venezia Giulia, located in northeastern Italy, once belonged to Austria and Slovenia, and the Italians in this area often speak German or Slovenian as their first language. Not surprisingly, the food is very different from that in other parts of Italy. Rather than pasta, cooks there make a variety of dumplings, and sauerkraut turns up in many dishes. The region is also famous for its excellent wines, especially the whites.

The creamy texture and buttery flavor of this soup from the region make it particularly comforting on a cold winter day. Cornmeal (polenta) is the unusual thickener for the soup. Kale or a combination of greens can be used in place of the spinach.

Serves 6

4 tablespoons (½ stick) unsalted butter

2 garlic cloves, minced

2 (10-ounce) bags spinach, washed, tough stems removed, and torn into bite-size pieces

5 cups Rich Vegetable Broth (page 88) or chicken broth

½ cup finely ground yellow cornmeal

Salt and freshly ground pepper

½ cup freshly grated Parmigiano-Reggiano

In a large pot, melt 3 tablespoons of the butter over medium heat. Add the garlic and cook, stirring, until lightly golden, about 1 minute. Stir in the spinach and cook until wilted, about 5 minutes. Add 4 cups of the broth and bring to a simmer.

Stir together the remaining 1 cup broth and the cornmeal in a small bowl until smooth. Add to the pot, stir well, and season to taste with salt and pepper. Cook, stirring occasionally, until the soup is thickened, about 30 minutes; if the soup becomes too thick, add some warm water and stir well.

Taste for seasoning. Stir in the remaining tablespoon of butter and the cheese and serve.

Lentil, Potato, and Spinach Soup

*T*his is my idea of a perfect year-round soup, since the vegetables in it are always in season and lentils and tomato paste are staples in my pantry. In the winter, I serve it hot accompanied by cheese and salumi, and in the summer, I serve it at room temperature with just a drizzle of extra-virgin olive oil.

Serves 4 to 6

1 celery rib, chopped

1 medium onion, chopped

1 carrot, peeled and chopped

1 teaspoon chopped fresh thyme

1 teaspoon chopped fresh rosemary

¼ cup extra-virgin olive oil, plus more (optional) for drizzling

2 garlic cloves, very finely chopped

8 ounces (about 1 cup) brown lentils

2 tablespoons tomato paste

5 cups water

2 medium waxy potatoes, such as Yukon Golds, peeled and chopped

Salt and freshly ground pepper

2 cups packed, washed, and trimmed spinach

In a large pot, cook the celery, onion, carrot, and herbs in the oil over medium heat, stirring often, until the vegetables are tender and golden, about 10 minutes. Stir in the garlic and cook for 1 minute.

Add the lentils and tomato paste and stir well. Add the water, potatoes, 1 teaspoon salt, and pepper to taste and bring to a simmer. Reduce the heat to low and cook for 45 minutes, or until the lentils and potatoes are tender. If the soup becomes too thick, add warm water.

Tear the spinach leaves into pieces and stir into the soup. Cook until wilted. Taste for seasoning.

Serve hot or at room temperature, drizzled with olive oil, if you like.

Farro-Vegetable Soup

*F*arro is a grain similar to wheat. It has a nutty flavor and chewy texture that contrast with the softness of the potatoes and the tasty strands of kale in this soup. Farro is sold whole, with the bran still attached; semi-pearled, with the bran partially removed; and pearled, with the bran completely removed. Whole farro has more fiber, but it takes longer to cook. Spelt, wheat berries, or barley can be substituted.

Escarole, Swiss chard, or cabbage can stand in for the kale in this soup.

Serves 4

1 medium onion, chopped

¼ cup extra-virgin olive oil

1 garlic clove, minced

2 medium potatoes, peeled and chopped

1 cup (about 6 ounces) pearled farro

6 cups water

Salt

8 ounces Tuscan or regular kale, trimmed and cut into ½-inch-wide strips

1 cup chopped canned Italian tomatoes

Pinch of crushed red pepper

⅓ cup freshly grated Pecorino Romano

In a large pot, cook the onion in the olive oil over medium heat, stirring often, until golden, about 8 minutes. Stir in the garlic and cook for 1 minute.

Add the potatoes and farro and cook for 10 minutes. Stir in the water and salt to taste, then stir in the kale, tomatoes, and red pepper. Bring to a simmer and cook for 30 minutes, or until the soup is thick and the potatoes and farro are tender; add more water if the soup becomes too thick.

Serve sprinkled with the cheese.

Celery-Rice Soup

*C*elery appears often in recipes but rarely gets to play a starring role. This soup is an exception, since the flavor of the celery is what defines it. The potatoes and rice have the supporting parts.

Serves 4

1 large onion, chopped

3 tablespoons extra-virgin olive oil

4 celery ribs, chopped

2 medium waxy potatoes, such as Yukon Golds, peeled and chopped

6 cups Rich Vegetable Broth (page 88) or chicken broth

½ cup long-grain white rice

Salt and freshly ground pepper

2 tablespoons chopped fresh parsley

½ cup freshly grated Parmigiano-Reggiano

In a large pot, cook the onion in the olive oil over medium heat until tender and golden, about 8 minutes. Add the celery and potatoes and stir well. Add the broth, bring to a simmer, and cook for 20 minutes, or until the vegetables are tender.

Stir in the rice and salt and pepper to taste, lower the heat, and cook, stirring occasionally, for 20 minutes, or until the rice is tender. Stir in the parsley.

Serve sprinkled with the cheese.

Barley and Leek Soup

*B*arley, called *orzo* in Italian, is believed to be one of the world's oldest cultivated foods. It became less important in the country as wheat and other grains began to replace it, but it is still used in many recipes from the Trentino-Alto Adige region in Northern Italy. Its nutty flavor and chewy texture are a welcome addition to soups, salads, sides, and *orzotto*, which is similar to risotto. Barley is also used to make a caffeine-free coffee substitute called *caffè d'orzo*, which is widely available in Italy.

Made with barley, mellow leeks, and a hint of thyme, this soup is a classic from Northern Italian kitchens.

Serves 4

2 medium leeks, trimmed, chopped, and well washed

1 celery rib, chopped

1 medium carrot, peeled and finely chopped

1 teaspoon chopped fresh thyme

3 tablespoons extra-virgin olive oil

1 cup barley

6 cups Rich Vegetable Broth (page 88) or chicken broth

Salt and freshly ground pepper

½ cup freshly grated Parmigiano-Reggiano

In a large pot, cook the leeks, celery, carrot, and thyme in the oil over medium heat, stirring often, until the vegetables are tender and golden, about 10 minutes.

Add the barley and broth and bring to a simmer. Reduce the heat to low and cook for 45 minutes, or until the soup is thickened and the barley is tender. If the soup is too thick, add a little warm water. Season to taste with salt and pepper.

Serve sprinkled with the cheese.

Cauliflower Soup
with Whole Wheat Ditalini

*O*n our way to visit my husband's family in Agrigento in Sicily, we stopped for lunch at the most famous and probably the best restaurant on the island, Il Duomo in Ragusa. The chef, Ciccio Sultano, is known for his personalized take on such Sicilian ingredients as local fish, sheep's-milk ricotta, pistachios, and wild fennel. The restaurant is small, with a classically Victorian décor. It looked as if it could have been the setting for a scene in Giuseppe Tomasi di Lampedusa's great novel about Sicily, *Il Gattopardo*. The service was formal and the food unique.

Later that day we arrived at my husband's cousin Marisa's house. Knowing we had probably eaten a big lunch, she was kind enough to make us a light evening meal consisting of a bowl of this simple soup made with fresh cauliflower from her garden and whole wheat pasta. We couldn't have asked for anything better.

Serves 4

3 large garlic cloves

¼ cup extra-virgin olive oil

1 small cauliflower (about 1 pound), trimmed, cored, and cut into bite-size pieces

Salt

3 cups Rich Vegetable Broth (page 88) or chicken broth

1 cup whole wheat ditalini or tiny shells

2 cups water

Freshly ground pepper

2 tablespoons chopped fresh parsley

½ cup freshly grated Pecorino Romano

In a large saucepan, cook the garlic in the oil over medium heat for 1 minute, or until lightly golden. Add the cauliflower and salt to taste and cook, stirring, for 2 minutes, or until it is coated with the oil.

Add the broth, bring to a simmer, and cook for 5 minutes. Stir in the pasta and water and cook for 10 minutes, or until the pasta is tender. If the soup is too thick, stir in more water. Season with pepper to taste.

Add the parsley and ¼ cup of the cheese. Serve sprinkled with the remaining ¼ cup cheese.

Autumn Vegetable Soup

I've never come across a winter squash soup that I didn't like, but this just might be my favorite. The squash is simmered with a potato, a bell pepper, and tomatoes, which give it a more complex flavor. I like to make it in the autumn when all of the vegetables in my market are locally grown and at their best. Crunchy croutons and a drizzling of olive oil are the final touches.

Serves 6 to 8

1 large onion, chopped

2 tablespoons extra-virgin olive oil, plus more for drizzling

1 butternut or other winter squash (about 2 pounds), halved lengthwise, seeded, peeled, and chopped (about 8 cups)

1 large waxy potato, such as Yukon Gold, peeled and chopped

1 small red bell pepper, chopped

1 cup chopped canned Italian or fresh tomatoes

4 cups Rich Vegetable Broth (page 88) or chicken broth, or more as needed

Salt and freshly ground pepper

1 recipe Croutons (page 89)

In a large pot, cook the onion in the oil over medium heat until tender and golden, about 10 minutes. Add the squash, potato, and bell pepper and stir well. Stir in the tomatoes, broth, and salt and pepper to taste and bring to a simmer. Cover the pot, reduce the heat, and cook for 30 minutes, or until the vegetables are tender. Remove from the heat and let cool slightly.

Transfer the soup to a blender or food processor and puree in batches if necessary. Return to the pot. If the soup is too thick, stir in more broth or water to taste. Season with salt and pepper to taste and reheat.

Serve the soup sprinkled with the croutons and drizzled with olive oil.

Holiday Chestnut Soup

For years I searched for the perfect starter for Thanksgiving or Christmas dinner. Once I tasted this elegant chestnut soup in Piedmont, I knew I had found it.

Creamy, smoky, and a bit piney from the rosemary, the soup is a perfect preface for any important dinner. It is perfectly delicious made with jarred roasted chestnuts. Many supermarkets and gourmet shops sell these, especially around the holidays, or see Sources (page 316).

Serves 6

1 medium onion, chopped

1 medium carrot, peeled and chopped

1 celery rib, chopped

3 tablespoons extra-virgin olive oil, plus (optional) more for drizzling

1 (14-ounce) jar peeled roasted chestnuts

1 (3-inch) sprig fresh rosemary

8 cups water

Salt and freshly ground pepper

1 recipe Croutons (page 89)

In a large pot, cook the onion, carrot, and celery in the oil over medium heat until tender and golden, about 10 minutes.

Stir in the chestnuts, rosemary, water, and 1 teaspoon salt and bring to a simmer, then reduce the heat to low and cook for 1 hour, or until the chestnuts are soft. Discard the rosemary sprig. Let cool slightly.

Transfer the soup to a blender or food processor in batches and puree until smooth. Return the soup to the pot, reheat, and season to taste with salt and pepper.

Ladle the soup into bowls, sprinkle with the croutons, and drizzle with a little olive oil, if you like.

Milanese Winter Squash Soup

*W*inter in Milan is often gray and damp. Feeling cold and tired on a visit there, I was looking for a pick-me-up and ordered this soup of the day for lunch at a busy trattoria. I was rewarded by its gorgeous orange color and creaminess. The addition of small pasta gave the soup more substance. Here's my version.

In Milan, the preferred cheese for this is Grana Padano, a locally made cow's-milk cheese that closely resembles Parmigiano-Reggiano. Both are firm-textured and flavorful, but Grana Padano is slightly milder and less crumbly.

Serves 4

1¼ pounds butternut or other winter squash, halved lengthwise, seeded, peeled, and chopped (about 5 cups)

2 cups water

2 cups milk

Salt

1 cup tubetti or ditalini pasta

2 tablespoons unsalted butter

¾ cup freshly grated Grana Padano or Parmigiano-Reggiano

In a large saucepan, combine the squash and water and bring to a simmer. Cover and cook for 15 to 20 minutes, or until the squash is very tender. Let cool slightly.

Transfer the soup to a blender or food processor in batches and puree until smooth. Return the soup to the saucepan. Whisk in the milk and salt to taste and bring to a simmer over medium heat. Add the pasta and cook, stirring often so that the pasta does not stick, until tender yet firm to the bite, about 10 minutes. Add more water if the soup is too thick.

Stir in the butter and ½ cup of the cheese. Taste for seasoning. Serve sprinkled with the remaining ¼ cup cheese.

Rich Vegetable Broth

*E*asy and inexpensive to make, this broth gets its rich flavor from the variety of vegetables, including meaty mushrooms. You will find it invaluable for all kinds of soups and risotto.

Makes 3 quarts

2 medium onions, chopped

4 celery ribs, sliced

4 medium carrots, peeled and sliced

2 tablespoons extra-virgin olive oil

1 medium tomato, halved

1 garlic clove, skin left on

1 (10-ounce) package cremini or white mushrooms or 6 dried shiitake mushrooms

2 sprigs fresh parsley

1 branch fresh thyme or ½ teaspoon dried

1 teaspoon black peppercorns

2 teaspoons salt

4 quarts water

In a large pot, cook the onions, celery, and carrots in the oil over medium heat, stirring often, until golden, about 10 minutes.

Add the tomato, garlic, mushrooms, parsley, thyme, peppercorns, salt, and water and bring to a boil, then reduce the heat to low so that the liquid just simmers and cook until slightly reduced, about 1½ hours. Let cool slightly.

Strain the broth into a bowl. Use immediately or let cool. Cover and refrigerate for up to 3 days. The broth can also be frozen in sealed containers for up to 3 months.

Croutons

*T*hese little squares of toasted bread add crunch to all kinds of soups and salads. They are so good that I often make a large batch and keep the leftovers to munch on.

Makes about 1½ cups

2 tablespoons extra-virgin olive oil

4 slices crusty white or whole wheat Italian bread, cut into ½-inch cubes

In a medium skillet, heat the oil over medium heat. Add the bread cubes and cook, tossing frequently, until golden and crisp, 5 to 6 minutes. Let cool completely. (*The croutons can be made up to 2 days ahead and stored in a plastic bag at room temperature.*)

VARIATION

Substitute butter for the olive oil.

Risotto, Farro, Legumes, and Polenta

Spring Risotto
with Asparagus, Peas, and Fontina

*H*ére are some of the myths about risotto: Making it takes a long time; you have to stand over a hot pot and stir constantly; risotto is hard to make.

Greatly exaggerated, I say. Preparing risotto the traditional way takes only about 20 minutes to cook from the time you add the rice to the pot. When I make risotto, I get it going and give it a stir. Then I turn and put some dishes in the sink, come back, stir, add some more broth, pour myself a glass of wine, stir, and add another dose of broth, check on whatever else is cooking, and repeat. Don't go too far, but there's no need to stand over it constantly.

This version captures the essence of spring with the fresh flavors of asparagus, peas, and scallions blended with creamy, tangy Fontina Valle d'Aosta.

Serves 6

12 ounces asparagus, trimmed

5 cups Rich Vegetable Broth (page 88) or chicken broth

2 tablespoons unsalted butter

1 tablespoon extra-virgin olive oil

1 medium onion, finely chopped

4 scallions, chopped

1½ cups short-grain rice, such as Arborio

½ cup dry white wine, at room temperature

Salt and freshly ground pepper

1 cup fresh or thawed frozen peas

1 cup grated Fontina Valle d'Aosta (see headnote, page 54)

⅓ cup freshly grated Parmigiano-Reggiano

Cut the tips off the asparagus and set them aside. Chop the asparagus stalks into ½-inch pieces.

In a medium saucepan, bring the broth just to a simmer over medium heat. Turn the heat to low to keep warm.

In a large wide saucepan, melt the butter with the olive oil over medium heat. Add the onion and cook until lightly golden, about 8 minutes. Stir in the scallions and cook for 1 minute. Add the rice and cook over medium-high heat, stirring often with a wooden spoon, for 3 minutes, or until the rice is hot and coated in oil and butter. Add the wine and cook, stirring, until it has evaporated.

Add the warm broth about ½ cup at a time, stirring frequently after each addition and waiting until each one is almost absorbed before adding more. Regulate the heat so that the liquid remains at a simmer and the rice does not dry out. After about 10 minutes, stir in the asparagus stems and continue cooking and adding broth. If you run out of liquid before the rice is done, add warm water. Season to taste with salt and pepper. When the risotto is almost ready—it will be firm yet tender to the bite and look creamy when it's done—16 to 18 minutes, stir in the asparagus tips and peas. Cook for 2 minutes more.

Stir in the cheeses and let stand for 1 minute, then spoon the risotto into shallow bowls and serve.

Risotto with Basil, Pine Nuts, and Parmesan

*B*asil, pine nuts, and cheese are also the primary ingredients in a classic pesto, but here the flavor combination is much more delicate and mellow. Shallots are used as the foundation for this risotto. Since they can burn easily, they are cooked with a little water to prevent them from browning before they are tender. This is a good trick taught to me by a chef friend, and it works just as well with sautéed onions.

Serves 6 to 8

5 cups Rich Vegetable Broth (page 88) or chicken broth

36 fresh basil leaves

¼ cup plus 2 tablespoons extra-virgin olive oil

Salt and freshly ground pepper

2 tablespoons water

3 medium shallots, finely chopped

2 cups short-grain rice, such as Arborio

½ cup dry white wine, at room temperature

⅔ cup freshly grated Parmigiano-Reggiano

2 tablespoons pine nuts, toasted and coarsely chopped

In a medium saucepan, bring the broth just to a simmer over medium heat. Turn the heat to low to keep warm.

Meanwhile, put 30 of the basil leaves in a blender or food processor and chop fine. Add ¼ cup of the oil and salt and pepper to taste and puree until smooth. Set aside.

Heat the remaining 2 tablespoons oil and the water in a large wide saucepan over medium heat. Add the shallots and cook until they are tender and the water has evaporated, about 5 minutes. Increase the heat to medium-high, add the rice, and cook, stirring often with a wooden spoon, for 3 minutes, or until the rice is hot. Add the wine and cook, stirring, until evaporated.

Add the warm broth about ½ cup at a time, stirring frequently after each addition and waiting until each one is almost absorbed before adding more. Regulate the heat so that the liquid remains at a simmer and the rice does not dry out. If you run out of liquid before the rice is done, add warm water. Season to taste with salt and pepper. The risotto is ready when it is firm yet tender to the bite and looks creamy, 18 to 20 minutes.

Stir in the basil puree. Tear up the remaining 6 basil leaves and add them, along with the grated cheese. Stir well.

Spoon the risotto into shallow bowls, sprinkle with the pine nuts, and serve.

Risotto with Sun-Dried Tomatoes, Arugula, and Ricotta Salata

~◦~

*T*he ingredients in this risotto—arugula, sun-dried tomatoes, and ricotta salata—are typical of the southern region of Puglia. Ricotta salata is a firm cheese made by pressing and drying fresh ricotta; if it is not available, substitute mild goat cheese or feta. I prefer to buy sun-dried tomatoes in their dry state, since the marinated ones often have too much seasoning. But if they are not available, use marinated—just rinse them well under warm water and blot them dry first.

Serves 4

5 cups Rich Vegetable Broth (page 88) or chicken broth

½ cup chopped sun-dried tomatoes (see headnote),

2 tablespoons unsalted butter

1 tablespoon extra-virgin olive oil, plus more for drizzling

4 scallions, chopped

1 cup short-grain rice, such as Arborio

Salt and freshly ground pepper

½ cup crumbled ricotta salata

1 cup chopped arugula

In a medium saucepan, bring the broth just to a simmer over medium heat. Turn the heat to low to keep warm. Place the tomatoes in a bowl and add ½ cup of the broth.

In a large wide saucepan, melt the butter with the olive oil over medium heat. Stir in the scallions and cook for 3 minutes, or until tender. Increase the heat to medium-high, add the rice, and cook, stirring often with a wooden spoon, for 3 minutes, or until the rice is hot.

Add the warm broth about ½ cup at a time, stirring frequently after each addition and waiting until each one is almost absorbed before adding more. Regulate the heat so that the liquid remains at a simmer and the rice does not dry out. After about 10 minutes, stir in the tomatoes and their broth and continue cooking and adding broth. If you run out of broth before the risotto is done, add warm water. Season to taste with salt and pepper. The risotto is ready when it is firm yet tender to the bite and looks creamy, 18 to 20 minutes.

Stir in the ricotta salata until melted, then stir in the arugula.

Spoon the risotto into shallow bowls, drizzle with a little extra-virgin olive oil, and serve.

Risotto with Leeks and Mushrooms

*T*he wild-mushroom season was at its height one fall in Piedmont when we stopped for dinner at Trattoria Anna. To celebrate the season, the menu of the day had fungi in every course. I was afraid the dinner might be monotonous, but each dish was different and special. I knew I couldn't get all of the kinds of mushrooms that were used in the risotto, but the waiter told me that leeks, onions, and garlic ensured it would be full of flavor. I make it with regular cultivated mushrooms and am pleased with the results.

Serves 6 to 8

5 cups Rich Vegetable Broth (page 88) or chicken broth

4 tablespoons (½ stick) unsalted butter

1 tablespoon extra-virgin olive oil

1 medium leek, trimmed, well washed, and chopped

1 small onion, finely chopped

8 ounces cremini or portobello mushrooms, cleaned, trimmed, and sliced

2 teaspoons finely chopped fresh sage or ½ teaspoon crumbled dried

1 garlic clove, very finely chopped

2 cups short-grain rice, such as Arborio

½ cup dry white wine, at room temperature

Salt and freshly ground pepper

½ cup freshly grated Parmigiano-Reggiano

In a medium saucepan, bring the broth just to a simmer over medium heat. Turn the heat to low to keep warm.

In a large wide saucepan, melt 2 tablespoons of the butter with the oil. Add the leek and onion and cook, stirring occasionally with a wooden spoon, until golden, about 10 minutes. Add the mushrooms and cook for 10 minutes, or until the juices they release have evaporated. Stir in the sage and garlic and increase the heat to medium-high. Stir in the rice and cook, stirring often, for 3 minutes, or until the rice is hot. Add the wine and cook, stirring, until it has evaporated.

Add the warm broth about ½ cup at a time, stirring frequently after each addition and waiting until each one is almost absorbed before adding more. Regulate the heat so that the liquid remains at a simmer and the rice does not dry out. If you run out of liquid before the risotto is done, add warm water. Season to taste with salt and pepper. The risotto is ready when it is firm yet tender to the bite and looks creamy, 18 to 20 minutes.

Stir in the remaining 2 tablespoons butter and the cheese. Spoon the risotto into shallow bowls and serve.

Risotto with Kale

*I*n Tuscany, kale is known as *cavolo nero*, meaning "black cabbage." It's a member of the brassica tribe, which includes cauliflower, broccoli, collard greens, cabbage, and Brussels sprouts. This is one healthy family! They all contain powerful chemicals that help prevent cancer.

Also known as lacinato kale, or dinosaur kale, because of its bumpy leathery-looking surface, the Tuscan variety is slightly sweeter than regular or curly kale. A bright, fresh bunch of it called to me at the farmers' market one day, and I decided to add it to risotto. We loved it. If there are still any kale doubters out there, this is a great way to introduce them to this green. If Tuscan kale is unavailable, regular kale can be substituted.

Serves 6

Salt

1 bunch kale (about 12 ounces), preferably Tuscan, trimmed

1 medium onion, finely chopped

¼ cup extra-virgin olive oil, plus more for drizzling

2 garlic cloves, finely chopped

1½ cups short-grain rice, such as Arborio

½ cup dry white wine, at room temperature

Freshly ground pepper

¾ cup freshly grated Parmigiano-Reggiano

Bring about 8 cups salted water to a boil in a large pot. Stack the kale leaves a few at a time and cut them crosswise into narrow strips. Add the kale to the boiling water and cook for 5 minutes, or until tender. Remove with a skimmer or slotted spoon and drain in a colander. Keep the cooking liquid warm over low heat.

In a large wide saucepan, cook the onion in the olive oil over medium heat, stirring occasionally, for 8 minutes, or until lightly golden. Stir in the garlic and cook for 1 minute. Increase the heat to medium-high, add the rice, and cook, stirring often with a wooden spoon, for 3 minutes, or until the rice is hot. Add the wine and cook until it has evaporated.

Add the kale cooking water about ½ cup at a time, stirring frequently after each addition and waiting until each one is almost absorbed before adding more broth. Regulate the heat so that the liquid remains at a simmer and the rice does not dry out. After about 10 minutes, stir in the kale and continue cooking and adding broth. If you run out of liquid before the rice is done, add warm water. Season to taste with salt and pepper. The risotto is ready when it is firm yet tender to the bite and looks creamy, 18 to 20 minutes.

Stir in the cheese and drizzle with a little oil. Spoon into shallow bowls and serve.

Risotto with Pears and Gorgonzola

*R*isotto made with fruit may sound odd, but it is delicious. Sweet pears and Gorgonzola cheese are a marriage made in risotto heaven. Be sure to use really ripe pears for maximum effect. To taste the fullness of the pears and cheese, I dilute the broth with water to lighten it.

Once you have tasted this risotto, try apple, strawberry, or orange risotto.

Serves 6

3 cups Rich Vegetable Broth (page 88) or chicken broth

2 cups water

3 tablespoons unsalted butter

1 tablespoon extra-virgin olive oil

1 medium onion, very finely chopped

1½ cups short-grain rice, such as Arborio

¾ cup dry white wine, at room temperature

2 large ripe Bartlett or Anjou pears, peeled, halved, cored, and finely chopped

Salt and freshly ground pepper

3 ounces Gorgonzola dolce, crumbled

In a medium saucepan, bring the broth and water just to a simmer over medium heat. Turn the heat to low to keep warm.

In a large wide saucepan, melt 2 tablespoons of the butter with the olive oil over medium heat. Add the onion and cook, stirring occasionally with a wooden spoon, until golden, about 8 minutes. Increase the heat to medium-high, add the rice, and cook, stirring often, for 3 minutes, or until the rice is hot. Add the wine and cook, stirring, until it has evaporated. Stir in the pears and cook for 1 minute.

Add the warm broth mixture about ½ cup at a time, stirring frequently after each addition and waiting until each one is almost absorbed before adding more. Regulate the heat so that the liquid remains at a simmer and the rice does not dry out. If you run out of liquid before the rice is done, add warm water. Season to taste with salt and pepper. The risotto is ready when it is firm yet tender to the bite and looks creamy, 18 to 20 minutes.

Stir in the remaining 1 tablespoon butter and the cheese, spoon into shallow bowls, and serve.

Farro with Brussels Sprouts, Sage, and Garlic

alvia, the Italian word for "sage," is derived from the Latin *salus*, meaning "health." Ancient people grew sage because they believed in its medicinal properties and its ability to enhance longevity. That's why when someone sneezes, an Italian will wish him or her long life by saying *Salute!*

The musky, minty flavor and aroma of sage is also welcome in the kitchen. The leaves are used to season game birds, turkey, or chicken, to cook beans, and to flavor focaccia. Italians even fry the fresh leaves whole in a light batter for an appetizer.

In this recipe, butter and sage work their magic on Brussels sprouts tossed with chewy farro. I like to serve it with baked fish.

Serves 4

10–12 ounces Brussels sprouts, trimmed and halved lengthwise

Salt

1½ cups (9 ounces) pearled farro (see headnote, page 79)

4 tablespoons (½ stick) unsalted butter

2 garlic cloves, chopped

6 sage leaves, chopped

Freshly ground pepper

¾ cup freshly grated Parmigiano-Reggiano or a blend of Parmigiano-Reggiano and Pecorino Romano

Bring a medium pot of water to a boil. Add the Brussels sprouts and salt to taste and cook for 3 to 5 minutes, or until the sprouts are almost tender. Remove with a slotted spoon.

Return the water to a boil, add the farro, and cook, stirring occasionally, for 20 minutes, or until tender. Drain well.

Melt the butter in a large skillet. Add the garlic and sage and cook over low heat for 2 minutes, or until fragrant; regulate the heat so that the butter does not brown. Add the Brussels sprouts and salt and pepper to taste and cook until the sprouts are tender, about 5 minutes.

Stir in the farro and half of the cheese. Transfer to a serving bowl, sprinkle the remaining cheese on top, and serve.

Farro, Zucchini,
and Sun-Dried Tomato Salad

*C*ombined with zucchini and sun-dried tomatoes, farro makes a delicious salad—something a little different for a summer barbecue or a picnic. If farro is unavailable, you can substitute wheat berries or spelt or even pearl barley. Although their flavors are not the same, their appearance and chewy texture are similar.

To make this salad in advance, prepare all the ingredients, but don't combine them until you're ready to serve so that they keep their bright freshness.

Serves 4

1½ cups (9 ounces) pearled farro (see headnote, page 79)

Salt

½ cup sun-dried tomatoes (not oil-packed), soaked in hot water for 10 minutes

½ small red onion, finely chopped

¼ cup shredded fresh basil

¼ cup chopped fresh parsley

1 tablespoon chopped fresh mint

¼ cup extra-virgin olive oil

2 tablespoons fresh lemon juice

1 tablespoon red wine vinegar

Freshly ground pepper

2 small zucchini, scrubbed, trimmed, and cut into small dice

Bring 6 cups water to a boil in a medium saucepan. Add the farro and 1 teaspoon salt and cook until the farro is tender, about 20 minutes. Drain and place in a serving bowl.

Meanwhile, drain the sun-dried tomatoes, pat dry, and chop into small dice.

Toss the farro with the onion, herbs, oil, lemon juice, vinegar, and salt and pepper to taste. Add the tomatoes and zucchini, toss well, and serve.

Warm Lentil and Vegetable Salad

This makes an excellent appetizer or summer main course, or serve it as a side dish with sausages or chops. Italians grow many types of lentils. Castelluccio lentils from Umbria and the Pantelleria variety from Sicily are two that I especially like because of their flavor and their thin skins, which make them more tender. But even ordinary supermarket lentils work for this salad, though you may need to cook them slightly longer.

Serves 4 to 6

1 tender celery rib, finely chopped

1 medium onion, finely chopped

1 medium carrot, peeled and finely chopped

½ teaspoon chopped fresh thyme

¼ cup extra-virgin olive oil

8 ounces (about 1 cup) lentils (see headnote)

1 large tomato, seeded and chopped, or 1 cup chopped canned Italian tomatoes

1 garlic clove, minced

Salt

1 large red bell pepper, chopped

Freshly ground pepper

In a large saucepan, cook the celery, onion, carrot, and thyme in the olive oil over medium heat until the vegetables are tender and golden, about 10 minutes.

Meanwhile, wash the lentils under running water. Look them over and discard any shriveled ones or foreign objects.

Stir the tomato and garlic into the vegetables. Add the lentils, 1 teaspoon salt, and 5 cups water and bring to a simmer. Cover, reduce the heat to low, and cook for 20 minutes.

Stir in the bell pepper. Cook for 20 to 30 minutes more, stirring occasionally, until the lentils are tender and most of the liquid has evaporated. If the lentils start to dry out, add a little more warm water as needed.

Add pepper to taste and more salt if needed. Serve warm or at room temperature.

Beans with Sage and Garlic

~~~

*C*anned beans are high on the list of convenience ingredients. So why bother to cook beans from scratch? There are so many reasons, I hardly know where to begin! Variety is a big one. There are all kinds of terrific and unusual dried beans that you won't find in a can. Have you tried *coco* (small, white, and creamy), *corona* (giant, white, and meaty), or *cicerchie* (like a flattened chickpea), for example? These are just three of the unique Italian legumes you can find only in their dried form. Look for them in specialty stores or online (see Sources, page 316).

Dried beans cost less than canned and, unlike the canned versions, are very low in sodium, so they are better for you. But the most important reason to cook your own beans is that they just taste better. Freshly cooked beans have flavor and texture that the canning process obliterates. Whether you cook them with vegetables or leave them plain to add to other recipes, you are in control of the flavors and seasoning.

Of course, you do have to plan ahead somewhat when making them, but it's easy to cook up a big batch. Let the beans cool and freeze them in small containers so you can pull them out whenever you like. And since beans can sometimes be unpredictable in their cooking time, it makes sense to prepare them ahead.

For the best results, soak the dried beans overnight. But a quick boil and short rest, known as the "quick-soak method," gives similar results.

Makes 6 cups

1 pound dried cannellini or borlotti (cranberry) beans or chickpeas

Salt

Optional (any or all)

2 garlic cloves

1 medium onion

1 medium carrot

1 celery rib

1 (3-inch) sprig fresh sage or rosemary

Wash the beans and look them over for any broken or shriveled ones or stones. Place them in a large bowl and cover them with several inches of cold water.

Refrigerate for at least 6 hours, or overnight.

Alternatively, for the quick-soak method, place the beans in a large pot, add water to cover by 2 to 3 inches, bring to a boil, and cook for 10 minutes. Turn off the heat and let soak for 1 hour.

Drain the beans and place them in a large pot. Discard any loose skins. Add cold water to cover by 1 inch, 1 teaspoon salt, and any or all of the optional seasonings. Bring to a simmer, partially cover, and cook the beans until tender, 1 to 1½ hours (longer if using chickpeas). If the liquid drops to the level of the beans, add more water to just cover. To test

for doneness, taste 2 or 3 beans: They should be tender and creamy. Let the beans cool in their liquid.

Discard the vegetables and herb sprig, if you used them, and add salt to taste. Use immediately, or store the beans in their liquid in the refrigerator or in individual containers in the freezer. They will keep in the refrigerator for up to 3 days or in the freezer for up to 4 months.

Kale and Cannellini Bean Stew

*E*scarole or broccoli rabe would also be good in this hearty stew. With cooked or canned beans on hand, it's the kind of easy dish you can put together in a hurry. For a complete meal, serve over rice or polenta or with crostini alongside.

Serves 6

2 garlic cloves, finely chopped

3 tablespoons extra-virgin olive oil

1 cup chopped fresh or canned Italian tomatoes

Pinch of crushed red pepper

Salt

4 cups cooked cannellini beans (see page 106) or two 16-ounce cans beans, with their liquid

6 cups chopped kale (see headnote)

In a medium pot, cook the garlic in the oil over medium heat until lightly golden, about 2 minutes. Add the tomatoes, red pepper, and a pinch of salt. Stir in the beans and cook for 10 minutes.

Add the kale and stir well. Cook for 15 minutes, or until the kale is wilted and tender. Taste for seasoning and serve.

Borlotti (Cranberry) Beans in Red Wine

*R*ed wine, vegetables, and herbs add big flavor to these beans. I serve them over slices of toasted bread, creamy polenta, or cooked rice, or as a side dish with pork or steak. Known as borlotti in Italy, cranberry beans have beautiful pink and white skins, though they turn a uniform beige as they cook. Their rich, meaty flavor goes especially well with the red wine in this recipe. Cannellini or Great Northern beans can be substituted.

Serves 6 to 8

1 small onion, finely chopped

1 celery rib, finely chopped

¼ cup extra-virgin olive oil

¾ cup dry red wine

½ cup chopped fresh or canned Italian tomatoes

1 (3-inch) sprig fresh rosemary or 1 teaspoon crumbled dried

Salt and freshly ground pepper

4 cups cooked dried borlotti (cranberry) beans (see headnote) or two 16-ounce cans beans, with their liquid

In a large saucepan, cook the onion and celery in the oil over medium heat until tender, about 8 minutes. Stir in the wine and bring to a simmer. Add the tomatoes, rosemary, and salt and pepper to taste and cook for 5 minutes.

Add the beans, with their liquid, to the simmering sauce and cook for 20 to 30 minutes, or until the sauce is thickened. Discard the rosemary sprig.

Taste for seasoning and serve.

Creamy Polenta Three Ways

$\mathcal{W}$hen I first learned to make polenta, I thought there was only one way to do it. The classic method involves standing and stirring the pot of boiling liquid as the cornmeal is ever so slowly blended in, and then continuing to stir until the mixture is creamy. The result was fantastic, but I had an aching back and occasional burns from scalding polenta splashing on my hand.

Now I cook polenta on the stovetop over very low heat, bake it in the oven, or simmer it in a slow cooker. All three of these methods are practically effortless and guaranteed to produce velvety polenta without aches or burns, but the slow-cooker version, which is from my book *The Italian Slow Cooker*, might just be my favorite of all. Once the polenta is cooked, you can leave it in the slow cooker on low so that it remains hot and creamy until you are ready to serve it.

Serves 6

1 cup coarsely ground yellow cornmeal
5 cups water
1 teaspoon salt, or to taste

For the no-stir stovetop method

Stir together the cornmeal and 1 cup of the water in a bowl. In a medium heavy saucepan, bring the remaining 4 cups water to a boil. Stir the cornmeal mixture into the boiling water, add the salt, and bring back to a boil. Cover the pot, reduce the heat to low, and cook, stirring occasionally, for 30 minutes, or until the polenta is creamy and there is no bitter taste. Taste for seasoning and serve.

For the oven method

Preheat the oven to 375°F.

Whisk together all of the ingredients in a 9-x-13-inch baking pan. Bake, uncovered, for 1 hour.

Remove the pan from the oven and whisk the polenta well. Place the pan back in the oven and bake for 10 minutes more, or until the polenta is thick. Taste for seasoning and serve.

For the slow-cooker method

In a large slow cooker, stir together the cornmeal, water, and salt. Cover and cook on high for 2 hours.

Stir the polenta. If it seems too thick, add a little more water. Cook for 30 to 60 minutes more, or until thick and creamy. Taste for seasoning and serve.

VARIATIONS

• Stir in butter and/or grated cheese when the polenta is done.

• Use half broth and half water.

• Use half milk and half water.

Fried Polenta with Mushrooms

*C*risp squares of golden polenta studded with mushrooms are crunchy on the outside and creamy within, just right with a glass of Barbera, a local red wine. One fall day, I ate them at Belvedere, a classic Piemontese restaurant overlooking the vineyards in one of Italy's greatest wine regions. When the waiter came to the table a little too soon to take away what remained on my plate, it was all I could do not to snatch it back from him.

I like to serve these with poached eggs for a special breakfast or with just about anything saucy, such as a stew.

Serves 6 to 8

2 tablespoons unsalted butter

3 tablespoons extra-virgin olive oil

1 small onion, chopped

8 ounces white mushrooms, cleaned, trimmed, and thinly sliced

1 teaspoon minced fresh sage or a pinch of crumbled dried

1 recipe Creamy Polenta (page 110), still hot

Oil a 13-x-9-x-2-inch baking dish. Melt the butter with 1 tablespoon of the oil in a large skillet over medium heat. Add the onion and cook, stirring occasionally, until tender and golden, about 10 minutes. Stir in the mushrooms and sage and cook, stirring often, until the mushrooms are lightly browned and the juices they release have evaporated.

Scrape the mushrooms into the cooked polenta and stir well. Spread the polenta evenly in the prepared baking dish. Let cool to room temperature. (*The polenta can be made ahead to this point. Cover and refrigerate for up to 2 days.*)

Cut the polenta into 2-inch squares. Heat the remaining 2 tablespoons oil in a nonstick skillet over medium-high heat. Add a few of the polenta squares and cook until golden brown, about 4 minutes. Turn the pieces and brown them on the other side. Drain on paper towels. Repeat with the remaining polenta.

Serve hot.

Pasta

Green Fettuccine
with Asparagus, Basil, and Butter

$\mathcal{T}$his green-on-green pasta is the essence of springtime, and I start to crave it as soon as the first crocuses appear. The combination of asparagus, nutty Parmigiano-Reggiano, and the delicate accent of basil is perfection.

In a recipe with just a few ingredients, it is important that all of them be top-notch. Even the butter, an ingredient we sometimes take for granted, should be the best. I am particularly fond of Kerrygold, which comes from Ireland and has more flavor than standard American brands.

As for the asparagus, thick spears benefit from peeling to make them more tender, skinny ones don't.

Serves 8

4 tablespoons (½ stick) unsalted butter

¼ cup chopped scallions

2 pounds asparagus, trimmed and cut into ½-inch pieces

Salt and freshly ground pepper

¼ cup water

1 pound Fresh Spinach Pasta (page 151), rolled out and cut into fettuccine

½ cup shredded fresh basil

¼ cup chopped fresh parsley

¾ cup freshly grated Parmigiano-Reggiano

In a large skillet, melt 2 tablespoons of the butter. Add the scallions and cook until softened, about 2 minutes. Add the asparagus, salt and pepper to taste, and the water, cover and cook, stirring occasionally, for 5 minutes, or until the asparagus is crisp-tender.

Meanwhile, bring a large pot of salted water to a boil.

Add the pasta, stir well, and cook, stirring often, until al dente. Scoop out some of the cooking water and set it aside. Drain the pasta.

Add the pasta to the pan with the asparagus, add the remaining 2 tablespoons butter, the basil, and parsley and toss well. If the pasta seems dry, stir in a little of the reserved cooking water.

Toss the pasta with half of the cheese, sprinkle the remaining cheese on top, and serve immediately.

Fettuccine with Roasted Pepper Sauce

*T*omatoes are not the only ingredient you can use to make a thick, rich red sauce for pasta. Here, butter and Parmesan heighten the sweet, smoky flavor of pureed roasted red peppers. You can roast the peppers up to 3 days ahead of time, then cook the sauce and pasta in minutes before serving. This sauce is inspired by one made by a Tuscan cook who served it over farro.

Serves 6 to 8

4 large red bell peppers, quartered, roasted, and peeled (see page 32)

Salt and freshly ground pepper

8 tablespoons (1 stick) unsalted butter, softened

1 recipe Fresh Egg Pasta (page 147), rolled out and cut into fettuccine

1 cup freshly grated Parmigiano-Reggiano

Place the peppers and their juices in a food processor or blender, season with salt and pepper to taste, and puree until smooth.

In a skillet large enough to hold all the ingredients, melt the butter over medium-low heat. Add the pepper puree and bring to a simmer.

Meanwhile, bring a large pot of salted water to a boil. Add the pasta, stir, and cook, stirring often, until al dente. Scoop out some of the cooking water and set aside. Drain the pasta.

Add the pasta to the sauce with a little of the cooking water and toss to coat. Add the cheese, toss well, and serve immediately.

Fettuccine with Lemon Cream

*I*n Sorrento, in Southern Italy, gigantic lemons grow everywhere. From pastas to pastry, cooks have dozens of ways to use them. This recipe is a favorite of mine when I am craving something rich. The sauce is made in minutes from lemon juice and zest, cream, butter, basil, and Parmigiano. Fresh fettuccine is my first choice here.

Serves 6 to 8

1 lemon, scrubbed

2 tablespoons unsalted butter

1 cup heavy cream

¼ cup minced fresh basil

Salt and freshly ground pepper

1 recipe Fresh Egg Pasta (page 147), rolled out and cut into fettuccine

1 cup freshly grated Parmigiano-Reggiano

Grate 1 teaspoon zest from the lemon. Halve the lemon and squeeze 2 tablespoons juice.

Melt the butter in a skillet large enough to hold all of the ingredients. Add the cream and lemon juice, bring to a simmer, and cook, stirring occasionally, until the sauce is slightly thickened, about 10 minutes. Stir in the lemon zest, basil, and salt and pepper to taste, remove from the heat, and cover to keep warm.

Meanwhile, bring a large pot of salted water to a boil. Add the fettuccine, stir well, and cook, stirring often, until al dente. Scoop out some of the cooking water and set aside. Drain the pasta.

Add the pasta to the sauce and toss well, adding a little of the cooking water if needed. Add the cheese, toss again, and serve immediately.

Spaghetti with Artichokes, Peas, and Eggs

I always keep a few packages of frozen vegetables in the freezer: Peas, spinach, and artichoke hearts are essentials. Not only are they handy to have when fresh seasonal vegetables are scarce, but they also enable me to make a quick dish like this one on short notice.

Serves 4

1 medium onion, finely chopped

¼ cup extra-virgin olive oil

1 (9-ounce) package frozen artichoke hearts, partially thawed and thinly sliced

½ cup water

Salt and freshly ground pepper

¾ cup frozen peas (not thawed)

8 ounces spaghetti

2 large eggs

½ cup freshly grated Pecorino Romano

In a skillet large enough to hold all of the ingredients, cook the onion in the oil over medium heat until softened, about 5 minutes. Add the artichokes, water, and salt and pepper to taste, cover, and cook for 10 minutes. Stir in the peas and cook for 2 minutes.

Meanwhile, bring a large pot of salted water to a boil. Add the spaghetti to the boiling water, stir, and cook, stirring frequently, until al dente.

In a small bowl, beat the eggs with ¼ cup of the cheese.

Scoop out some of the pasta cooking water and set aside. Drain the pasta and toss it into the skillet with the vegetables. Add a little of the cooking water, drizzle with the egg mixture, and toss well until the spaghetti is coated with the sauce.

Sprinkle with the remaining ¼ cup cheese and serve immediately.

Spaghetti Calabrese with Pancetta, Bell Pepper, and Tomato Sauce

Calabria is Italy's ground zero for hot chiles. Everybody with access to a bit of soil grows them, whether in big plots, backyards, or flower boxes. When fresh, the chiles are eaten raw in salads or sprinkled on pasta. In the fall, the plants are tied into bundles and hung in the sun to dry, to use in stews and soups.

This rustic pasta includes both sweet bell peppers and a fresh chile. I use jalapeños because they are easy to find and available year-round. Pancetta (cured pork belly) or guanciale (salt-cured pork cheek) is often used in this sauce, but you can substitute bacon or leave out the pork if you prefer.

Serves 6 to 8

Salt

2 medium red bell peppers, halved and seeded

2 cups chopped canned Italian tomatoes

3 tablespoons extra-virgin olive oil

4 ounces pancetta, guanciale, or bacon, chopped

2 garlic cloves, minced

1 tablespoon minced jalapeño or a pinch of crushed red pepper

1 pound spaghetti

6–8 large fresh basil leaves, torn

½ cup freshly grated Pecorino Romano

Bring a large pot of salted water to a boil. Add the pepper halves and cook for 2 minutes, until slightly softened. Remove the peppers with a slotted spoon. Turn off the heat but reserve the water to cook the pasta.

Pat the peppers dry and cut them into 4 or 5 pieces each. Put them in a blender or food processor, along with the tomatoes, and puree until smooth.

In a skillet large enough to hold all of the ingredients, heat the oil over medium heat. Add the pancetta and cook for 8 to 10 minutes, or until golden. Stir in the garlic and cook for 2 minutes, or until softened.

Add the pepper mixture, jalapeño, and salt to taste, bring the sauce to a simmer, and cook for 10 minutes, or until slightly thickened.

Meanwhile, bring the reserved water back to a boil. Add the spaghetti, stir, and cook, stirring frequently, until al dente.

Drain the spaghetti and add to the sauce, along with the basil. Toss well.

Sprinkle with the cheese and serve immediately.

Shoemaker's Spaghetti

I've heard various explanations for why this Neapolitan pasta is attributed to shoemakers. The most logical one is that the busy workers at a shoe factory in Naples had little time and few ingredients at hand at mealtimes, and this speedy sauce was one that they could cook up in a jiffy.

At first glance, the ingredients seem familiar, but what makes this dish special is that the pasta is added to the sauce when slightly underdone, and so it becomes infused with the flavors of the sauce as it finishes cooking. Once the cheese is stirred in, the sauce becomes even creamier.

I like to use the imported canned cherry tomatoes known as *piennolo* tomatoes. They are becoming more widely available here (see Sources, page 316), and they are perfect for quick sauces like this one. If you can't find them, use fresh cherry or grape tomatoes instead.

Serves 4 to 6

Salt

1 large garlic clove, cut in half

Pinch of crushed red pepper

3 tablespoons extra-virgin olive oil

1 (14-ounce) can imported cherry tomatoes with juices (see headnote) or 2 cups cherry or grape tomatoes, quartered

¼ cup water if using fresh tomatoes

12 ounces spaghetti

3 tablespoons freshly grated Pecorino Romano

3 tablespoons freshly grated Parmigiano-Reggiano

4 fresh basil leaves, torn into 2 or 3 pieces each

Bring a large pot of salted water to a boil.

Meanwhile, in a skillet large enough to hold all of the ingredients, cook the garlic and red pepper in the oil over medium heat until the garlic is golden, about 2 minutes. Add the tomatoes and salt to taste; if using fresh tomatoes, add the water. Bring to a simmer over medium heat and cook, stirring occasionally and crushing the tomatoes with the back of a spoon, until the sauce is thickened, about 10 minutes. Discard the garlic.

Once the water comes to a boil, add the pasta, stir, and cook, stirring often, until almost but not quite al dente. Scoop out some of the cooking water and set aside. Drain the pasta.

Add the cheeses to the simmering sauce, with a little of the cooking water, and stir until the cheese melts. Add the pasta to the sauce, tossing and turning it to coat completely. Cook, stirring gently, until the pasta is al dente.

Add the basil and serve immediately.

Spaghetti alla Spaghettata
(with Red Wine, Garlic, and Olives)

*W*hen Italians crave a midnight snack or other impromptu meal, it is time for a *spaghettata*, meaning a "spaghetti party." A *spaghettata* calls for something very fast and uncomplicated, with lively flavors that jump off the plate and into your mouth. It has to be made with ingredients on hand: There is no time to shop.

For a *spaghettata perfetta*, this recipe can't be beat. It's a variation on the theme of *aglio e olio*, garlic and oil sauce. In this version, red wine stains the pasta a rosy color, while the garlic, olives, and hot pepper give it a punch. Like most *aglio e olio* pastas, it does not call for cheese.

Serves 2 to 4

2 large garlic cloves, thinly sliced

2 tablespoons chopped fresh parsley

Pinch of crushed red pepper

¼ cup extra-virgin olive oil

½ cup thinly sliced pitted imported black olives

Salt

8 ounces spaghetti or linguine

1 cup dry red wine

In a skillet large enough to hold all of the ingredients, cook the garlic, parsley, and red pepper in the oil over medium heat until the garlic is lightly golden, about 3 minutes. Stir in the olives and cook for 5 minutes.

Meanwhile, bring a large pot of salted water to a boil. Add the pasta, stir, and cook, stirring often, until almost, but not quite al dente. Drain.

While the pasta is cooking, turn the heat under the skillet to high, add the wine, and bring to a boil.

Add the spaghetti to the skillet and cook, stirring, until al dente, about 2 minutes more. Serve immediately.

VARIATION

Add some chopped anchovies, canned tuna, or capers with the olives.

Whole Wheat Linguine
with Kale and Chickpeas

*T*his dish was inspired by one I enjoyed in Puglia. Cicerchia (chee-*cher-kee-ah*), an unusual legume that resembles a flat chickpea, had been simmered with wild chicory and tossed with whole wheat linguine. My version includes meaty kale and easily available chickpeas, which I cook with garlic and hot pepper. The nutty flavor and chewy, somewhat coarse texture of whole wheat or farro linguine complement the chickpeas and vegetables perfectly.

Serves 6 to 8

Salt

12 ounces kale, trimmed

2 large garlic cloves, finely chopped

Pinch of crushed red pepper

⅓ cup extra-virgin olive oil, plus more for drizzling

2 cups drained cooked chickpeas (see page 106), or drained canned chickpeas

1 pound whole wheat or farro linguine

½ cup freshly grated Pecorino Romano

Bring a large pot of salted water to a boil. Add the kale and cook for 5 minutes. Remove the kale with a slotted spoon, or tongs; reserve the cooking water to cook the pasta. Let the kale cool, then chop it into small pieces.

In a deep skillet large enough to hold all of the ingredients, cook the garlic and red pepper in the oil over medium heat for 1 minute, or until the garlic is golden. Add the chickpeas and cook, stirring, for 5 minutes. Stir in the kale and a pinch of salt, lower the heat, and cover the pan. Cook for 10 minutes more, or until the kale is tender. Add a little of the cooking water if the sauce seems dry.

Meanwhile, return the vegetable cooking water to a boil. Add the pasta, stir well, and cook, stirring often, until al dente. Drain.

Add the pasta to the chickpeas and the kale, turn the heat up to high, and toss well. Add the cheese and toss again.

Serve immediately, drizzled with a little extra-virgin olive oil.

"Angry" Sicilian Pasta

$\mathcal{W}$hat's so angry about this summery pasta? A touch of crushed red pepper fires it up, "enraging" the combination of herbs, tomatoes, and cheese tossed with bow tie pasta. I can't imagine a more appealing dish for a warm summer night.

Grating garlic on a Microplane is easier and faster than chopping it, and the even texture that results allows it to blend in better with the other ingredients. And a Microplane is a lot easier to clean than a garlic press.

Serves 6

2 large ripe tomatoes, chopped

½ cup shredded fresh basil

¼ cup capers, rinsed and patted dry

¼ cup chopped fresh spearmint

2 tablespoons chopped fresh oregano

1 garlic clove, grated (see headnote) or minced

¼ teaspoon crushed red pepper

⅓ cup extra-virgin olive oil

Salt

1 pound bow tie pasta

½ cup freshly grated Pecorino Romano

In a large serving bowl, toss together the tomatoes, basil, capers, mint, oregano, garlic, red pepper, and olive oil. Season to taste with salt. (*The sauce can be made up to 1 hour ahead of time. Cover and let stand at room temperature.*)

Meanwhile, bring a large pot of salted water to a boil. Add the pasta, stir well, and cook, stirring frequently, until al dente. Scoop out some of the cooking water and reserve. Drain the pasta.

Add the pasta to the bowl, with a little of the reserved cooking water if needed, and toss well. Add the cheese and toss again. Serve hot or warm.

Bow Ties with Mushrooms and Tomatoes

*M*y father had an old friend who came from Abruzzo, in central Italy, and loved to go foraging for wild mushrooms. He had been trained in mycology, the study of mushrooms, and every spring and fall, when the weather was just right, he would go out to the woods near his home in New Jersey and look for different varieties that were in season. From time to time, he would bring us a big bagful, every one carefully inspected to be sure that it was safe to eat.

My mother often used them in soups and sautés, but one of my favorite ways to have them was in a sauce for pasta. This is my version of a mushroom sauce I had at the home of winemaker friends in Tuscany. I like it with a chunky pasta shape, such as bow ties, that complements the appearance and texture of the mushroom slices and bits of tomato.

A mix of mushrooms, such as cremini, shiitake, oyster, and button, creates the best flavor for this sauce.

Serves 6 to 8

1 medium red onion, finely chopped

¼ cup extra-virgin olive oil

2 garlic cloves, finely chopped

2 teaspoons chopped fresh thyme

12 ounces mixed mushrooms (see headnote), cleaned, trimmed (if using shiitakes, discard the stems), and sliced

Salt and freshly ground pepper

2 medium fresh tomatoes, chopped, or 1 cup chopped canned Italian tomatoes

2 tablespoons chopped fresh parsley

1 pound bow tie pasta

2 tablespoons unsalted butter

½ cup freshly grated Parmigiano-Reggiano

In a skillet large enough to hold all of the ingredients, cook the onion in the olive oil over medium heat, stirring often, until tender and golden, about 8 minutes. Stir in the garlic and thyme and cook for 1 minute. Add the mushrooms and salt and pepper to taste and cook, stirring often, until the mushrooms are tender and the juices they release evaporate, about 10 minutes. Stir in the tomatoes, parsley, and more salt and pepper to taste. Cook for 5 minutes, or until the tomatoes are soft.

Meanwhile, bring a large pot of salted water to a boil. Add the pasta, stir well, and cook, stirring frequently, until al dente. Scoop out some of the cooking water and set aside. Drain the pasta.

Add the pasta to the sauce, with the butter and a little of the cooking water, and toss well. Stir in the cheese and serve immediately.

One-Pot "Dragged" Penne

*T*he first time I saw the name of this dish, *strascicata*, on a restaurant menu, I was sure that my less-than-perfect knowledge of Italian had failed me. *Strascinare* means "to drag," an odd thing to do to pasta. But the waiter explained that the chef had cooked the pasta in the sauce, stirring, or "dragging," it and adding more liquid as it cooked. The technique is similar to making risotto. The pasta becomes infused with the sauce and develops a creamy texture from the starch it releases as it is stirred.

Like risotto, this method does require a fair amount of stirring, so plan to stay close to the stove. On the up side, you will need to wash only one pot.

Serves 4

1 cup Marinara Sauce (page 171)

8 ounces penne

About 2 cups water

Salt

½ cup freshly grated Parmigiano-Reggiano

Heat the sauce in a 10-inch skillet over medium heat. Add the penne and stir to coat with the sauce. Stir in 2 cups water and bring to a simmer. Cook, stirring frequently, until the sauce is reduced and thickened and the pasta is al dente; if necessary, add more water to prevent the pasta from sticking. Add salt to taste.

Stir in the cheese and serve immediately.

Penne with Zucchini and Herbs

*A*n *agriturismo* is a working farm that welcomes guests for get-away-from-it-all vacations. When I stayed at San Felice in Tuscany, we spent our days walking in the fields, watching the workers make cheese from their sheep's milk, and enjoying the experience of life on a farm. Every evening, Anna, the cook, would prepare simple meals featuring olive oil from their own trees and produce from the organic garden. One night she served us bowls of pasta and zucchini coated with an aromatic green sauce. When I asked her about it, she just shrugged and said that she makes it from whatever looks good in the garden.

Though my terrace will never yield the variety of produce that Anna's kitchen garden did, I can make my own version of her pasta with the dill and basil that I grow and fresh zucchini from the nearby farmers' market.

If you have a mortar and pestle, you can pound the herbs, garlic, and olive oil together the traditional way, but a food processor does an excellent job too.

Serves 6 to 8

2 tablespoons coarsely chopped fresh dill

½ cup shredded fresh basil

2 garlic cloves

½ cup extra-virgin olive oil

Salt and freshly ground pepper

4 medium scallions, chopped

1½ pounds zucchini, scrubbed, trimmed, and cut into 1½-x-½-inch thick strips (like French fries)

1 pound penne

¾ cup freshly grated Pecorino Romano

Place the dill, basil, and garlic in a food processor and chop them fine. Add ¼ cup of the oil and process until blended. Season to taste with salt and pepper.

Meanwhile, in a skillet large enough to hold all of the ingredients, cook the scallions in the remaining ¼ cup oil over medium heat until wilted, about 3 minutes. Add the zucchini and salt and pepper to taste. Cook for 10 minutes more, or until tender.

Meanwhile, bring a large pot of salted water to a boil. Add the pasta, stir well, and cook, stirring often, until al dente. Scoop out some of the cooking water and set aside. Drain the pasta.

Add the pasta to the skillet and toss well. Add the herb mixture and cheese and toss until blended. Add a little of the cooking water if the pasta seems dry. Serve immediately.

Seven-P Pasta

*W*hen I visited the Selvapiana winery in the Chianti region of Tuscany, I asked the cook about some of her favorite local dishes, and she was kind enough to share this one. She called it *pasta con sette P*—"seven-P pasta." The Ps stand for the ingredients: *porro* (leek), *pancetta* (unsmoked bacon), *peperoncino* (hot pepper), *pomodori* (tomatoes), *panna* (cream), penne, and Parmigiano-Reggiano.
   Now I make it often, though sometimes I leave out the pancetta.

Serves 6

3 ounces pancetta, chopped (optional)

1 medium leek, trimmed, split lengthwise, washed well, and cut into thin slices

Pinch of crushed red pepper

2 tablespoons extra-virgin olive oil

2 cups peeled, seeded, and chopped fresh tomatoes or chopped drained canned Italian tomatoes

Salt

½ cup heavy cream

1 pound penne or other tubular pasta

¾ cup freshly grated Parmigiano-Reggiano

In a skillet large enough to hold all of the ingredients, cook the pancetta (if using), leek, and red pepper in the oil over medium heat, stirring occasionally, until the leek is tender, about 10 minutes. Stir in the tomatoes and a pinch of salt, bring to a simmer, and cook over medium-low heat for 10 minutes, or until the sauce is thickened. Stir in the cream and bring to a simmer.

Meanwhile, bring a large pot of salted water to a boil. Add the pasta, stir well, and cook, stirring frequently, until al dente. Scoop out some of the cooking water and set aside. Drain the pasta.

Add the pasta and cheese to the sauce and toss well. Add a little of the cooking water if needed to loosen the sauce. Serve immediately.

Penne with Butternut Squash and Bacon

*W*hen I visited the Barilla Culinary Center in Parma, the chef showed me how he makes this pasta dish from the region. I was surprised to see that he used smoked bacon, which isn't common in Italy, but the salty touch was just right with the sweet squash.

Serves 4

2 ounces thick-sliced bacon, finely chopped

2 tablespoons extra-virgin olive oil

1 small red onion, finely chopped

1 teaspoon finely chopped fresh rosemary

1 garlic clove, finely chopped

3 cups diced peeled butternut squash

¼ cup water

Salt and freshly ground pepper

8 ounces penne

⅔ cup freshly grated Parmigiano-Reggiano

In a skillet large enough to hold all the ingredients, cook the bacon in the olive oil over medium heat until lightly golden, about 5 minutes. Add the onion and rosemary and cook for 8 minutes, or until the onion is tender.

Stir in the garlic and cook for 1 minute. Add the squash, water, and salt and pepper to taste, stir well, cover the pan, and cook, stirring occasionally, for 15 to 20 minutes, until the squash is tender and starting to brown. If it begins to stick, add another tablespoon or two of water. With the back of a spoon, mash some of the squash until creamy.

Meanwhile, bring a large pot of salted water to a boil. Add the pasta, stir well, and cook, stirring often, until al dente. Scoop out some of the pasta cooking water and set it aside. Drain the pasta.

Add the pasta to the squash mixture, with a little of the cooking water, and stir well. Cook, stirring, for 1 minute to coat the pasta.

Stir in the cheese and serve immediately.

Whole Wheat Fusilli
with Spicy Escarole, Tomatoes, and Olives

*W*hole wheat pasta isn't meant for delicate sauces, but I love its nutty flavor and slightly coarse texture with a chunky, garlicky sauce like this one. Escarole is a versatile green of which Southern Italians are especially fond. Uncooked, it makes a fine salad green. Cooking it brings out its slight sweetness. It can be stir-fried, added to soup, or tossed with pasta, as here.

Serves 6 to 8

Salt

1½ pounds escarole, trimmed and cut into bite-size pieces

2 large garlic cloves, thinly sliced

Pinch of crushed red pepper

¼ cup extra-virgin olive oil, plus more for drizzling

2 cups halved cherry tomatoes

½ cup chopped pitted imported black olives

1 pound whole wheat fusilli

½ cup freshly grated Pecorino Romano

Bring a large pot of salted water to a boil. Add the escarole and cook for 7 to 9 minutes, until the thick stems are tender. Remove with a slotted spoon. Drain well. Reserve the cooking water for the pasta.

In a skillet large enough to hold all of the ingredients, cook the garlic and red pepper in the oil over medium heat until the garlic is golden, about 5 minutes. Stir in the tomatoes and olives and cook for 10 minutes, or until the tomatoes are soft. Stir in the escarole and cook for 5 minutes; add a little warm water if the sauce seems dry.

Meanwhile, return the escarole cooking water to a boil. Add the pasta, stir well, and cook, stirring often, until al dente. Drain.

Add the pasta to the sauce, turn the heat to high, and toss the pasta well. Add the cheese and toss again. Drizzle with a little olive oil and serve immediately.

Whole Wheat Fusilli
with Broccoli and Olive Paste

*J*arred olive paste is handy to have in the pantry. (You can find it with the olives in most supermarkets, or see Sources, page 316.) Spread it on crostini or add it to salad dressing and sauces. One day, I stirred some into a garlicky broccoli sauce for whole wheat pasta. It added a twist to one of my favorite pastas.

Serves 6 to 8

Salt

1 medium bunch broccoli, trimmed and cut into small florets

2 large garlic cloves, thinly sliced

Pinch of crushed red pepper

¼ cup extra-virgin olive oil

2 tablespoons black olive paste (see headnote)

1 pound whole wheat fusilli

½ cup freshly grated Pecorino Romano

Bring a large pot of salted water to a boil. Add the broccoli and cook for 5 minutes, or until barely tender. Remove the broccoli with a slotted spoon and drain well. Leave the water at a boil for the pasta.

In a skillet large enough to hold all the ingredients, cook the garlic and red pepper in the olive oil over medium heat until the garlic is golden, about 2 minutes. Stir in the olive paste and broccoli, cover, and cook until the broccoli is tender, about 8 minutes. Taste for seasoning.

Meanwhile, add the pasta to the broccoli cooking water, stir well, and cook, stirring often, until al dente. Scoop out some of the cooking water and set aside. Drain the pasta.

Add the pasta to the skillet, with a little of the cooking water, and toss with the broccoli. Add the cheese, toss again, and serve immediately.

Rotelle with Spicy Cauliflower Ragu

*H*ome Food is an organization of Italians who enjoy cooking. Known as *Cesarine*, they are passionate about their local food and welcome guests into their homes for a meal of traditional foods. This is an exceptional opportunity to meet people, learn about Italian culture, and enjoy a home-cooked meal at a moderate price, especially if you are in an unfamiliar city.

We enjoyed a Home Food dinner in the home of a *Cesarina* in Catania. She received us like old friends, shared information about the city that only a native would know, told us a little about her family and her interesting life, and demonstrated a few of her recipes, including this one, in her warm and cozy kitchen. For more information about Home Food, go to www.homefood.it.

Rotelle or fusilli is the perfect pasta for this sauce. The crumbles of cauliflower simmered with garlic and tomatoes get caught in the ridges and loops, so every bite delivers their flavor. Sicilians like to add anchovies to the sauce, but if you prefer to leave them out, it will still be delicious.

Serves 4

Salt

1 medium cauliflower (about 2 pounds), trimmed, cored, and cut into florets

2 large garlic cloves, finely chopped

¼ cup extra-virgin olive oil, plus more for drizzling

6 anchovy fillets, drained and chopped (optional)

Pinch of crushed red pepper

1 (28-ounce) can Italian tomatoes, with their juice, chopped

½ teaspoon dried oregano

8 ounces rotelle or fusilli

Bring a large pot of salted water to a boil. Add the cauliflower and cook for 15 minutes, or until very tender when pierced with a knife.

Meanwhile, in a skillet large enough to hold all of the ingredients, cook the garlic in the oil over medium heat for 1 minute. Stir in the anchovies (if using) and red pepper and cook, stirring, until the anchovies are dissolved. Stir in the tomatoes, with their juice, oregano, and salt to taste and cook, stirring occasionally, until the tomatoes are slightly thickened, about 15 minutes.

When the cauliflower is very tender, scoop out the pieces with a slotted spoon and drain them well in a colander. Reserve the boiling water for the pasta. Add the cauliflower to the tomato sauce. With a large spoon, crush the cauliflower into the simmering sauce and cook for 10 minutes more.

Meanwhile, bring the cauliflower water back to a boil. Add the pasta, stir well, and cook, stirring often, until al dente. Drain.

Add the pasta to the sauce, tossing well to coat, drizzle with a little extra-virgin olive oil, and serve immediately.

Orecchiette with Potatoes and Arugula

*A*rugula is ideal as a salad green, but that doesn't mean it's not good cooked. In Puglia, it is used in soups and pasta sauces and sautéed as a side dish.

This recipe pairs orecchiette, little ear-shaped pasta, with arugula and potatoes. For the sauce, the potatoes turn creamy as they cook in the same pot with the pasta, and the pasta and vegetables get an added lift from sautéed garlic and a hint of hot pepper.

Serves 6

Salt

2 large garlic cloves, finely chopped

Pinch of crushed red pepper

⅓ cup extra-virgin olive oil, plus more for drizzling

2 medium waxy potatoes, such as Yukon Golds, peeled and cut into ½-inch dice

1 pound orecchiette

8 ounces arugula, washed and trimmed

Bring a large pot of salted water to a boil.

Meanwhile, in a skillet large enough to hold all of the ingredients, cook the garlic and red pepper in the oil over medium heat until the garlic is golden and fragrant, about 1 minute. Remove from the heat.

Add the potatoes to the boiling water. When the water is boiling again, stir in the pasta and cook, stirring occasionally, until the potatoes are tender and the pasta is al dente. Stir in the arugula. Scoop out some of the cooking water and set aside. Drain the pasta.

Place the skillet over medium heat, add the pasta and vegetables, and toss well. Add a little of the cooking water if the pasta seems dry. Drizzle with extra-virgin olive oil and serve immediately.

Eggplant Lasagna

⁓

*T*hink of this recipe as the offspring from the marriage of eggplant Parmesan and lasagna: They are made for each other. It's a traditional recipe from Naples and one that deserves to be better known. It serves a crowd, so it is perfect as a main dish for a big holiday meal.

Serves 8

2 medium eggplants (about 1 pound each), trimmed and cut into ¼-inch-thick slices

⅓ cup extra-virgin olive oil, plus more for brushing

1 medium onion, finely chopped

5 pounds plum tomatoes, peeled, seeded, and chopped, or two 28-ounce cans Italian tomatoes, chopped

Salt and freshly ground pepper

¼ cup shredded fresh basil

1 recipe Fresh Egg Pasta (page 147), rolled out into sheets and cut into 12-inch lengths

1 pound fresh mozzarella, quartered and cut into thin slices

1 cup freshly grated Parmigiano-Reggiano

Place racks in the upper and lower thirds of the oven and preheat the oven to 450°F.

Generously brush the eggplant slices on both sides with oil. Arrange the slices in a single layer on two large baking sheets. Bake the eggplant for 30 minutes, or until tender and lightly browned. Remove from the oven; reduce the heat to 375°F.

Meanwhile, in a large saucepan, cook the onion in the ⅓ cup olive oil over medium heat, stirring, until tender but not browned, about 10 minutes. Add the tomatoes and salt and pepper to taste, bring to a simmer, and cook until the sauce is slightly thickened, 15 to 20 minutes. Stir in the basil.

Lay out some kitchen towels on a work surface. Fill a large bowl with cold water. Bring a large pot of salted water to a boil.

Add a couple of pasta sheets to the boiling water. Remove them after 1 minute, or when they are still firm, and place in the bowl of water to cool, then lay them out flat on the towels. Repeat, cooking and cooling the remaining pasta in the same way; the towels can be stacked one on top of the other.

Lightly oil a 13-x-9-x-2-inch baking pan. Spread a thin layer of sauce in the pan. Top with a layer of pasta, slightly overlapping the sheets. Spread with a thin layer of sauce, then top with half of the eggplant slices, half of the mozzarella slices, and ⅓ cup of the grated cheese. Add another layer of pasta and spread with a thin layer of sauce. Top with the remaining eggplant slices, the remaining mozzarella slices, and ⅓ cup of the grated cheese. Top with a final layer of pasta, tomato sauce, and the remaining ⅓ cup grated cheese. (*The lasagna can be assembled up to 24 hours in advance, covered with plastic wrap, and refrigerated; remove from the refrigerator about 1 hour before baking.)*

Bake the lasagna for 45 minutes, or until the top is browned and the sauce is bubbling around the edges. If the lasagna is browning too much, cover it loosely with foil. Remove from the oven and let stand for 15 minutes.

Cut the lasagna into squares and serve.

Mushroom Ravioli with Pine Nut, Butter, and Sage Sauce

Woodsy mushrooms and creamy ricotta fill these little pasta pillows from Liguria, in northwestern Italy. I serve them with a butter sauce flavored with pine nuts and fresh sage.

When cooking ravioli, be sure to regulate the water so that it boils gently and does not cause the pasta to burst.

Serves 8

Ravioli

3 tablespoons unsalted butter

1 tablespoon extra-virgin olive oil

1 pound mushrooms, such as cremini, chanterelles, or portobellos, cleaned, trimmed, and thinly sliced

1 tablespoon chopped fresh marjoram or thyme or ½ teaspoon dried

Salt and freshly ground pepper

½ cup whole- or part-skim-milk ricotta

1 cup freshly grated Parmigiano-Reggiano

1 large egg yolk

Flour for dusting

1 recipe Fresh Egg Pasta (page 147), rolled out and trimmed into 4-inch-wide strips

To make the ravioli

In a large skillet, melt the butter with the oil over medium heat. Add the mushrooms, marjoram, and salt and pepper to taste and cook, stirring occasionally, until the mushrooms are tender and the juices they release have evaporated. Let cool.

Scrape the mushrooms into a food processor and finely chop. Scrape them into a large bowl. Stir in the ricotta and ½ cup of the grated cheese and taste for seasoning. Stir in the egg yolk. Cover and refrigerate while you make the ravioli.

Sprinkle a couple of baking sheets lightly with flour and set aside.

Lay one strip of the dough on a lightly floured surface. (Keep the others covered with plastic wrap.) Fold it lengthwise in half to mark the center, then unfold it. Beginning about 1 inch from one end, place a teaspoonful of the filling on the dough. Continue to place teaspoonfuls of the filling about 1 inch apart in a straight row down one side of the fold. Dip your finger lightly in cool water and run it around the filling to moisten the dough slightly, then fold the dough over the side with filling. Press out any air bubbles and seal the edges. Use a fluted pastry wheel or a sharp knife to cut between the dough-covered mounds of filling. Separate the ravioli and press the edges firmly with the back of a fork to seal. Place the ravioli in a single layer on one of the floured baking sheets.

continued on page 146

Repeat with the remaining dough and filling. Cover with a towel and refrigerate until ready to cook, or up to 3 hours, turning the pieces several times so that they do not stick to the pans. (*The ravioli can be frozen on the baking sheets until firm, then placed in a heavy-duty plastic bag, sealed tightly, and frozen for up to 1 month; do not thaw before cooking.*)

Just before serving, bring a large pot of salted water to a boil.

Sauce

12 tablespoons (1½ sticks) unsalted butter

¼ cup pine nuts or sliced almonds

8 fresh sage leaves

Salt

Meanwhile, make the sauce

In a saucepan, melt the butter with the pine nuts, sage, and a pinch of salt.

Lower the heat under the pot of boiling water so that the water boils gently. Add the ravioli and cook until tender, 2 to 5 minutes, depending on whether or not they were frozen. Scoop the ravioli out of the pot with a slotted spoon and drain well in a colander.

Pour half of the sauce into a warm serving bowl. Add the ravioli. Spoon on the remaining sauce, sprinkle with the remaining ½ cup Parmigiano-Reggiano, and serve immediately.

Fresh Egg Pasta

*T*here is nothing like homemade pasta. Flour and eggs come together to form tender, rich, and silky dough that you can roll out into sheets for lasagna, cut into fettuccine, or stuff and fold into ravioli. Once you get the knack of it, making pasta is a very satisfying skill. Plus, it costs a fraction of store-bought "fresh" pasta (which can be months old), and it has no additives or preservatives.

I like to make pasta dough by hand or in a heavy-duty mixer. Each method has its merits. Feeling and touching the dough enables you to judge when the balance of flour and eggs is just right, but using a mixer is a lot neater and makes short work of kneading the heavy dough. I don't recommend using a food processor, since it tends to heat up the dough and toughen it.

Once the dough is ready, you can roll it out with a hand-cranked pasta machine or an electric-powered roller (I have one that attaches to my heavy-duty mixer) or by hand with a rolling pin. The rolling pin does a great job, but it takes patience to get the pasta thin and even. I don't like the texture of the pasta that results from the extruding machines I've tried.

Makes about 1 pound

---

4 large eggs, beaten

2 teaspoons olive oil

About 3 cups unbleached all-purpose flour

To make the dough in a heavy-duty mixer

Put the eggs and olive oil into the bowl of the mixer fitted with the flat beater. With the mixer on low, add the flour a little at a time, stopping when the dough forms a ball around the beater and cleans the sides of the bowl. Pinch the dough: It should feel moist but not sticky. If it is sticky, add a little bit more flour as needed.

Turn the dough out onto a lightly floured surface and knead for 1 minute, or until the dough forms a neat ball with no streaks of flour.

To make the dough by hand

Mound the flour on a work surface. With your fingertips, make a wide crater in the center of the mound of flour. Pour in the eggs and oil and begin stirring with a fork, gradually incorporating the flour from the inside of the crater. Use your other hand to stabilize the wall of flour and prevent it from collapsing as you stir. When most of the flour has been incorporated and the dough forms a ball and becomes too firm to stir, push the remaining flour to one side. Lightly flour your hands and begin kneading, pushing the dough away from you with the heels of your hands and pulling it back toward you with your fingertips. Continue kneading, gradually incorporating some of the remaining flour, until the ball becomes somewhat smooth and feels moist but only slightly sticky. Do not add more flour than necessary, or the dough will become too dry. Continue kneading for 8 to 10 minutes, or until there are no streaks of flour in the dough and the color is evenly yellow.

With either method, set the dough aside and cover it with an over-turned bowl to prevent it from drying out. Let it rest for at least 30 minutes. Meanwhile, scrape the work surface to remove any scraps of dough.

To roll out the dough with a pasta machine

Set up the pasta machine, set the rollers at the widest opening, and dust them lightly with flour.

Cut the dough into 4 to 6 pieces. Work with 1 piece at a time, keeping the remainder covered.

Flatten a piece of dough into an oval disk. Turn the handle of the pasta machine with one hand and guide the piece of dough through the rollers with the other. If the dough sticks, ripples, or tears, dust it lightly with flour. Fold the dough crosswise into thirds. Pass it through the machine again, flouring it if necessary. Make a third pass in the same way.

Move the dial to the next notch and pass the dough through the rollers. As the dough emerges, lift it straight out so that it stays flat, without wrinkling (do not fold it this time). Continue to pass the dough through the machine, moving the dial one notch each time, until the desired thinness is reached. This will vary according to the machine, but I usually stop at the second-to-the-last setting for fettuccine, lasagna, and other flat pastas and the last notch for stuffed pasta. The pasta should be thin enough that you can see your hand through it without tearing. (Don't be tempted to reroll scraps of dough. Hardened edges can stick in the machine and tear the pasta.)

Lay the strip of dough on a lightly floured kitchen towel. Roll out the remaining dough in the same way, making all of the strips of equal thickness.

Turn the finished strips often so that they do not stick. If the dough will be used to make stuffed pasta, such as ravioli, keep it covered so that it remains pliable and use as soon as possible.

To roll out the dough by hand

Cut the dough into 4 to 6 pieces. Work with 1 piece at a time, keeping the remainder covered.

Lightly dust a clean work surface with flour. Shape a piece of dough into a disk. Dust a long wooden rolling pin with flour. Place the pin on the dough and roll it away from you toward the edge. Rotate the dough a quarter turn, center the pin on it, and push toward the edge once more. Repeat rotating and rolling the dough out from the center, keeping the shape round and the thickness even. Flip the dough over from time to time to be sure it is not sticking. Dust it lightly with flour if needed, but don't use so much flour that the dough dries out. The dough is thin enough when you can easily see your hand through it when it is held up to the light. Lay the dough on a lightly floured kitchen towel. Roll out the remaining dough in the same way.

If the dough will be used to make stuffed pasta, such as ravioli, keep it covered so that it remains pliable and use as soon as possible.

To cut the dough with a pasta machine

Following the manufacturer's instructions, pass each sheet of dough through the cutters. As the dough emerges, lift it straight out with your other hand so that the strands do not collect on the countertop and become wrinkled. (For a manual machine, it helps to have an assistant—that way, one can pass the dough through the cutters and lift it out while the other turns the crank.) Place the strands on a floured surface.

To cut the dough by hand

Let the dough dry until it is slightly leathery but still pliable, about 20 minutes.

Cut the dough into 10-inch lengths with a large heavy chef's knife. Loosely roll up a strip of dough and cut it crosswise into strips 4 inches wide for lasagna or ¼ inch wide for fettuccine. Separate the strips and place them flat on a floured surface to dry for about 1 hour at room temperature.

To store fresh egg pasta

The pasta can be used immediately, frozen, or allowed to dry completely before storing. To freeze the pasta, place the strips on baking sheets lightly dusted with flour so that they do not touch and place the baking sheets in the freezer. When the pasta is firm, gently gather fettuccine into a bundle or stack lasagna sheets. Wrap the pasta well in layers of plastic wrap or foil. Freeze for up to 1 month.

To dry the pasta, place the strips, not touching, on lightly floured baking sheets and cover with lightweight kitchen towels. (Do not cover them with plastic or foil, or they will turn moldy.) Leave the strips at room temperature for up to several days, until the pieces are completely dry and snap when broken. Store in plastic bags in the pantry until ready to use.

Fresh Spinach Pasta

 asta made with fresh spinach has a bright green color and a verdant flavor.

Makes about 1¼ pounds

1 pound spinach, rinsed and trimmed

¼ cup water

3 large eggs, beaten

3 cups unbleached all-purpose flour

Place the spinach in a large pot with the water. Cover and cook over medium heat for 5 minutes, or until the spinach is wilted and tender.

Drain the spinach and let cool. Place the spinach in a towel and squeeze out the liquid. Chop the spinach fine (you should have about ¾ cup).

Combine the spinach and eggs in a medium bowl, mixing well.

Mound the flour on a work surface. With your fingertips, make a wide crater in the center of the flour and pour in the spinach mixture. Begin stirring with a fork, gradually incorporating the flour from the inside of the crater. Use your other hand to stabilize the wall of flour and prevent it from collapsing. Continue as directed in Fresh Egg Pasta page 147.

Baked Spaghetti Frittata with Broccoli Rabe and Smoked Mozzarella

*I*n Naples, spaghetti and beaten eggs are mixed with broccoli rabe and smoked mozzarella, poured into a pan, and baked into a golden pasta frittata. Served hot or at room temperature, this is a great dish for a party or picnic. Smoked scamorza, a cow's-milk cheese, is similar to mozzarella but firmer and drier.

Serves 6 to 8

Salt

1 pound broccoli rabe, trimmed

12 ounces spaghetti

6 large eggs

¾ cup freshly grated Pecorino Romano

Freshly ground pepper

8 ounces smoked mozzarella or smoked scamorza, thinly sliced

Preheat the oven to 350°F. Bring a large pot of salted water to a boil. Oil a shallow 2-quart baking dish.

Add the broccoli rabe to the boiling water and cook for 5 to 8 minutes, until almost tender. Remove with a strainer; leave the water boiling. Let the broccoli rabe cool slightly, then chop it into bite-size pieces.

Add the pasta to the boiling water, stir well, and cook, stirring often, until almost but not quite al dente. Drain.

Meanwhile, in a large bowl, beat the eggs with ½ cup of the grated cheese, a pinch of salt, and pepper to taste. Add the pasta and toss well. Add the broccoli rabe and toss again.

Pour half of the mixture into the baking dish. Place the mozzarella on top. Add the remaining pasta. Sprinkle with the remaining ¼ cup grated cheese.

Bake for 25 to 30 minutes, or until the eggs are just set and the top is lightly browned. Serve hot or at room temperature, cut into wedges or squares.

Bow Ties Baked
with Cauliflower and Cheese

*B*ig baroque-looking heads of cauliflower, some creamy white and others tinged with pink, were piled high in the markets in Sicily one fall, so I wasn't at all surprised to find them included in our lunch when I visited the home of a family of cheese makers near Ragusa. After touring their immaculate small dairy and tasting their creamy ricotta, we sat down to steaming bowls of pasta baked with fresh cauliflower just harvested from a neighbor's garden. The mild cauliflower is the perfect foil for the sharpness of Pecorino and the creaminess of ricotta.

Serves 6 to 8

1 large onion

¼ cup plus 2 tablespoons extra-virgin olive oil

1 medium cauliflower, trimmed and chopped into ½-inch pieces (about 5 cups)

Salt and freshly ground pepper

12 ounces farfalle

1 (15-ounce) container whole-milk ricotta

1 cup freshly grated Pecorino Romano

½ cup plain dry bread crumbs

Preheat the oven to 400°F. Oil a 13-x-9-x-2-inch baking dish.

In a large skillet, cook the onion in ¼ cup of the oil over medium heat, stirring often, until golden, about 5 minutes. Add the cauliflower and salt and pepper to taste, stir well, cover, and cook, stirring occasionally, until the cauliflower is tender and just beginning to brown, about 15 minutes. Remove from the heat.

Meanwhile, bring a large pot of salted water to a boil. Add the pasta, stir well, and cook, stirring frequently, until almost but not quite al dente. Scoop out ½ cup of the cooking water and pour it into a large bowl. Drain the pasta.

Whisk the ricotta into the hot pasta water. Stir in the pasta. Spread half of the pasta in the baking dish. Spoon the cauliflower mixture over the pasta. Sprinkle with ½ cup of the grated cheese. Spread the remaining pasta on top.

Toss the bread crumbs with the remaining 2 tablespoons oil. Add the remaining ½ cup grated cheese and salt to taste and sprinkle the mixture over the pasta.

Bake for 20 minutes, or until the crumbs are golden and the pasta is heated through. Serve hot.

Baked Pasta Fagioli

*V*icolo della Neve ("Little Street of the Snow") is a restaurant and pizzeria in Salerno that is said to be two hundred years old. It got its name from the ice sellers who once populated the neighborhood in the days before refrigeration. My husband and I loved everything we ate there, from the sweet bell peppers stuffed with eggplant to the perfect Neapolitan-style pizzas. But the dish that made us swoon was the pasta fagioli baked in the blazing-hot pizza ovens. It tasted a lot like the traditional version that my mother used to make, but with a crunchy topping and crispy edges.

You can substitute cannellini or white kidney beans if borlotti are not available.

Serves 8

2 celery ribs, finely chopped

3 garlic cloves, finely chopped

¼ cup plus 2 tablespoons extra-virgin olive oil

2 cups tomato puree

Salt

Pinch of crushed red pepper

4 cups cooked borlotti (cranberry) beans (see headnote; see page 106), with their liquid

12 ounces mostaccioli or ziti

Preheat the oven to 375°F.

In a large saucepan, cook the celery and garlic in ¼ cup of the oil over medium heat until golden, about 5 minutes. Stir in the tomato puree, 1 teaspoon salt, and the red pepper, bring to a simmer, and cook for 5 minutes, or until slightly thickened.

Add the beans and their liquid, bring to a simmer, and cook for 5 minutes. Mash some of the beans with the back of a large cooking spoon or with a potato masher.

Meanwhile, bring a large pot of salted water to a boil. Add the pasta, stir well, and cook, stirring often, until almost but not quite al dente. Scoop out 2 cups of the cooking water. Drain the pasta.

Toss the pasta with the bean sauce and the reserved cooking water. It will look soupy. Spoon into a shallow 2½-quart baking dish. Drizzle with the remaining 2 tablespoons oil.

Bake for 45 minutes, or until the sauce is bubbling and the pasta is lightly browned on top. Serve hot.

Two-in-One Penne
with Mushrooms and Cream

*T*his recipe is a two-in-one because you can serve the pasta simply with the mushroom and cream sauce or take it a step further and bake it into a luscious casserole. In Piedmont, in northwestern Italy, porcini, or *cèpe*, mushrooms are used, but they are quite expensive here, so I choose a mix of flavorful cultivated varieties. The one thing I don't compromise on is the Fontina Valle d'Aosta, a semi-soft cow's-milk cheese from Northern Italy that has a mushroomy flavor and a smooth, creamy texture.

Serves 8

3 tablespoons unsalted butter

¼ cup chopped shallots

1 garlic clove, chopped

2 pounds mixed mushrooms, such as portobello, shiitake, and button, cleaned, trimmed (if using shiitakes, discard the stems), and cut into thick slices

Salt and freshly ground pepper

1 cup heavy cream, plus ¼ cup if baking the pasta

1 pound penne

8 ounces Fontina Valle d'Aosta (see headnote, page 54), thinly sliced

⅓ cup freshly grated Parmigiano-Reggiano

Melt the butter in a large skillet over medium heat. Add the shallots and cook until softened, about 3 minutes. Add the garlic and cook for 1 minute. Stir in the mushrooms and salt and pepper to taste and cook, stirring often, until the mushrooms begin to release their liquid. Turn the heat down slightly and cook until the liquid has evaporated and the mushrooms are lightly browned, about 10 minutes. Stir in the 1 cup cream and turn off the heat.

Meanwhile, bring a large pot of salted water to a boil. Add the pasta, stir well, and cook, stirring frequently, until al dente. Drain.

Add the pasta to the mushrooms and toss well.

To serve the pasta immediately, add the Fontina and toss well. Sprinkle with the grated cheese and serve.

Alternatively, preheat the oven to 400°F. Butter a 13-x-9-x-2-inch baking dish.

Spoon about one third of the pasta into the baking dish. Arrange half of the Fontina slices over the pasta. Make a second layer of pasta and top with the remaining sliced cheese. Spread the remaining pasta over the top and drizzle with the remaining ¼ cup cream. Sprinkle with the grated Parmesan.

Cover the baking dish with foil. Bake for 20 minutes. Uncover and bake for 10 minutes more, or until the sauce is bubbly and the top is golden. Serve hot.

Pasta Torta

For this savory torta, leftover pasta and sauce and a layer of mozzarella—either smoked or plain—or provolone or other meltable cheese are packed into a baking pan liberally coated with butter and bread crumbs and baked. After a brief rest, the beautiful golden torta is slipped out of the pan and served. With its brown crunchy edges and the designs formed by the pasta shapes, this looks and tastes so good, nobody will guess that you created it from leftovers.

Practically any pasta shape and sauce will do, though I like pasta with tomato sauce best, since the sauce keeps the pasta moist. This is a recipe that doesn't need exact measurements. If you like, add a little chopped ham or salami. Just don't let the cheese touch the sides of the pan, or it will prevent the torta from unmolding neatly.

Since I don't usually have leftover pasta, I sometimes double a recipe I'm making and refrigerate half to use for the torta later in the week.

Serves 6

3 tablespoons plain dry bread crumbs

3 large eggs

½ cup freshly grated Parmigiano-Reggiano

5–6 cups cooked pasta with tomato sauce (see headnote)

1 cup chopped cooked vegetables, such as peas, spinach, or broccoli (optional)

4 ounces mozzarella, imported Italian provolone, or Asiago, shredded

Preheat the oven to 375°F. Generously butter a 9-x-9-x-2-inch baking pan. Sprinkle the sides of the pan with 2 tablespoons of the bread crumbs, turning the pan to coat it evenly. Tap out the excess.

In a large bowl, whisk the eggs until blended. Beat in the Parmesan. Add the pasta and sauce and the vegetables, if using, and stir well.

Spoon half of the pasta into the pan, being careful not to disturb the crumbs. Sprinkle with the shredded cheese, avoiding the sides of the pan. Spoon on the remaining pasta and smooth the surface. Sprinkle with the remaining 1 tablespoon bread crumbs.

Bake the pasta for 50 minutes, or until golden brown on top and hot in the center. Remove from the oven and let stand for 10 minutes to allow the pasta to set.

Run a small knife around the edges of the pan. Invert the torta onto a serving plate. (If the pasta does not slip out of the pan, spoon it out—and butter the pan more generously next time.) Cut into squares and serve.

Cavatelli with Erice Pesto and Eggplant

*W*hen I stayed in Erice, a medieval town perched on a hilltop in western Sicily, a thick fog swirled through the streets one night as six of us made our way to a tiny trattoria. The menu was limited, so we all ordered the same pasta. Soon the waiter stepped out of the tiny kitchen carrying a huge bowl of *busiati*, a homemade fresh pasta similar to cavatelli, with a sauce prepared from uncooked tomatoes pounded with almonds, cheese, garlic, and basil, all topped with fried cubes of eggplant and rounds of potatoes. We dug in with enthusiasm. You can serve the pasta with just the pesto, but I love it with the eggplant. Back home I came up with this version.

Serves 6 to 8

Vegetable oil for frying

8 ounces small potatoes, peeled and cut into ¼-inch-thick slices

Salt

1 medium eggplant (about 1 pound), trimmed and cut into ½-inch cubes

3 garlic cloves

½ cup almonds (with skins)

½ cup packed fresh basil leaves

1 pound ripe tomatoes, cored and coarsely chopped

¾ cup freshly grated Pecorino Romano

⅓ cup extra-virgin olive oil

Freshly ground pepper

1 pound fresh or frozen cavatelli or dried pasta such as fusilli

Preheat the oven to 200°F.

Pour about 1 inch of vegetable oil into a deep skillet and heat over medium-high heat until very hot. Pat the potato slices dry with paper towels and slip some of them into the hot oil in a single layer. Fry, turning once, until golden brown on both sides and tender when pierced, about 10 minutes. Drain on paper towels. Sprinkle with salt. Repeat with the remaining potato slices. Keep warm in the oven.

Add only enough of the eggplant pieces to the hot oil to fit without crowding and cook, stirring occasionally, until nicely browned on all sides, about 15 minutes. With a slotted spoon, transfer to paper towels to drain. Cook the remaining eggplant in the same way. Keep warm in the oven.

Bring a large pot of salted water to a boil.

Meanwhile, finely chop the garlic in a food processor. Add the almonds and basil and chop fine. Add the tomatoes, cheese, and olive oil and process to a coarse puree. Season to taste with salt and pepper.

Add the pasta to the boiling water, stir well, and cook, stirring frequently, until it is al dente. Scoop out some of the cooking water and set aside. Drain the pasta.

Pour the pasta into a large serving bowl. Add the pesto and toss well. Add a little of the cooking water if needed to loosen the sauce. Add the eggplant and toss again. Scatter the potatoes on top and serve immediately.

Pumpkin Gnocchi alla Romana

*R*oman-style gnocchi are made with semolina flour and baked with butter and cheese. Here is a variation on that theme, with pureed pumpkin or another winter squash. The vegetable gives a warm color and mild sweetness to the gnocchi. Canned pumpkin or frozen squash puree makes a good shortcut, or you can use your own homemade puree.

I can't think of a better dish for an autumn dinner party. Make these a day or two ahead of time, then bake them just before you are ready to serve.

Serves 6

4 cups whole milk

Salt

1¼ cups water

1¼ cups semolina flour (Cream of Wheat)

8 tablespoons (1 stick) unsalted butter

4 large egg yolks

1 cup canned unsweetened pumpkin or cooked mashed butternut squash

⅛ teaspoon freshly grated nutmeg

1½ cups freshly grated Parmigiano-Reggiano

6 fresh sage leaves, chopped

Freshly ground pepper

Oil a large baking sheet.

In a medium saucepan, bring the milk and 2 teaspoons salt to a simmer.

Meanwhile, in a bowl, whisk together the water and semolina. Pour the mixture into the hot milk and cook, stirring with a wooden spoon, until the mixture is very thick, about 4 minutes. Remove from the heat, add 4 tablespoons of the butter, and stir until melted.

In a small bowl, beat together the egg yolks, pumpkin, and nutmeg. Beat the mixture into the semolina. Stir in 1 cup of the cheese.

Pour the mixture onto the baking sheet. With a spatula, spread it out evenly to ½ inch thick and smooth the top. Refrigerate for 3 hours, or until the semolina is firm to the touch. (*The dough can be covered and refrigerated overnight.*)

Preheat the oven to 400°F. Butter a 13-x-9-x-2-inch baking dish.

With a small knife, cut the dough into 2-inch squares. Slide a spatula under the squares and transfer them to the baking dish, overlapping them slightly.

Melt the remaining 4 tablespoons butter in a small saucepan, add the sage leaves and a pinch of salt, and cook for 1 minute, or until fragrant. Drizzle the butter over the gnocchi and sprinkle with pepper. Top with the remaining ½ cup cheese.

Bake for 30 minutes, or until the gnocchi are golden on top. Serve hot.

Basil-Ricotta Gnocchi
with Tomato-Butter Sauce

*L*ight and delicate gnocchi made with ricotta and flecked with fresh basil are a far cry from the more familiar, heavier potato gnocchi. Their flavor reminds me of the filling for good cheese ravioli. Paired with a buttery fresh tomato sauce, they are heavenly.

To make gnocchi that are light, not dense, drain the ricotta to eliminate excess liquid so that you won't have to add too much flour to compensate.

Serves 6

1 (15-ounce) container ricotta, preferably whole-milk

1 large egg

1 large egg yolk

6 fresh basil leaves, slivered

½ cup freshly grated Parmigiano-Reggiano, plus more for serving

½ teaspoon salt

Freshly ground pepper

About 1½ cups unbleached all-purpose flour

1 recipe Fresh Tomato-Butter Sauce (page 168), heated

Place the ricotta in a strainer lined with cheesecloth set over a bowl. Drain for at least several hours, or overnight, in the refrigerator.

In a large bowl, beat the egg and yolk until blended. Add the ricotta, basil, Parmesan, salt, and pepper to taste and stir well. Add 1 cup of the flour and stir just until combined. Sprinkle some of the remaining flour on a work surface. Turn the dough out and very gently turn it in the flour. Handle it lightly, adding only as much flour as needed to make a soft dough. Cut the dough into quarters. Set aside, covered with an overturned bowl.

Rinse and dry your hands and scrape the work surface clean. Line a large baking sheet with foil and dust it with flour. Dust the work surface with flour.

Roll one quarter of the dough into a 1-inch-thick log. Cut it into ½-inch slices. Arrange the slices on the baking sheet so that they do not touch. Repeat with the remaining dough. Place the baking sheet in the refrigerator until ready to use. (*The gnocchi can be refrigerated overnight or frozen for up to 1 month. To freeze, place the baking sheet in the freezer and freeze until firm, then transfer the gnocchi to a freezer bag, seal tightly, and freeze.*)

Bring a large pot of salted water to a boil. Have a large heated bowl ready.

Drop half of the gnocchi a few pieces at a time into the boiling water so that they do not stick together and stir gently. Lower the heat so that the water is just simmering. When the gnocchi rise to the surface, cook for 30 seconds more.

Pour half of the sauce into the heated bowl. Remove the gnocchi from the boiling water with a slotted spoon and place them in the sauce. Spoon on half of the remaining sauce. Cover and keep warm. Cook and drain the remaining gnocchi, add to the bowl, and top with the rest of the sauce.

Sprinkle with cheese and serve immediately.

Beet and Ricotta Gnocchi
with Gorgonzola Cream Sauce

*G*nocchi made from potatoes or ricotta may be the most familiar, but there are many other kinds found throughout Italy. Spinach gnocchi in Rome, mushroom gnocchi in the Alto Adige, and bread gnocchi in the Tyrol are just a few of the kinds I have enjoyed.

Made by kneading together a bit of flour and whatever else was on hand, gnocchi were probably created as a sort of desperation dinner, when times were hard and people were hungry. The name alone, which means "lumps" in Italian, seems to indicate that they were not very special. Now, enriched with cheese or coated with sauce, they make a luxurious addition to any meal.

The prizewinner for the prettiest gnocchi I have ever eaten were the brilliant pink gnocchi made with beets and ricotta I had in the town of Ravenna, in the Emilia-Romagna region. I serve them on top of a creamy Gorgonzola sauce so that their gorgeous color shines.

Serves 6 to 8

1 (15-ounce) container whole- or part-skim-milk ricotta

2 medium red beets (about 3 ounces each), roasted and peeled (see Note on page 18)

1 large egg

1 cup freshly grated Parmigiano-Reggiano, plus more for serving

Salt and freshly ground pepper

About ⅔ cup unbleached all-purpose flour, plus more for dredging

2 tablespoons unsalted butter

1 recipe Gorgonzola Cream Sauce (opposite page), heated

Place the ricotta in a strainer lined with cheesecloth set over a bowl. Drain for at least several hours, or overnight, in the refrigerator.

Cut the beets into chunks. Place them in a food processor and puree. Add the ricotta, egg, Parmesan, and salt and pepper to taste. Pulse until smooth. Transfer to a large bowl. Add ⅔ cup flour and stir to blend, adding more only if needed. Don't handle the dough any more than necessary, or it will become tough.

Line a large baking sheet with foil and dust it with flour. Lightly dust a dish with flour. Scoop up a tablespoonful of the dough and, with a second spoon, push it off into the dish. Roll the dough lightly in the flour and place it on the baking sheet. Repeat with the remaining dough, leaving space between the gnocchi on the sheet. (*The gnocchi can be refrigerated overnight or frozen for up to 1 month. To freeze, place the baking sheet in the freezer and freeze until firm, then transfer to a freezer bag, seal tightly, and freeze.*)

Bring a large pot of salted water to a boil. Have a large heated bowl ready. Place the butter in the bowl and let it melt, swirling it to coat the bowl. Keep warm.

Drop half of the gnocchi a few at a time into the boiling water so that they don't stick together and stir gently. Lower the heat so the water is just simmering. When the gnocchi rise to the surface, cook for 30 seconds more. Remove the gnocchi with a slotted spoon and transfer them to the bowl. Cover and keep warm. Cook and drain the remaining gnocchi and add to the bowl.

Spoon a little of the hot sauce onto each plate. Top with the gnocchi. Sprinkle with Parmesan and serve immediately.

Gorgonzola Cream Sauce

This lusciously rich sauce is my first choice for Beet and Ricotta Gnocchi (opposite page), but it is also good on just about any type of fresh pasta.

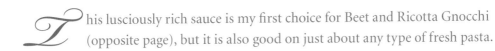

Makes about 2 cups

1 cup heavy cream
½ cup whole milk
8 ounces Gorgonzola dolce
Pinch of freshly grated nutmeg
Salt and freshly ground pepper

In a medium saucepan, bring the cream and milk to a simmer and cook for 5 minutes, or until slightly reduced. Reduce the heat to low and stir in the Gorgonzola until melted. Season with the nutmeg and salt and pepper to taste and serve.

Sauces, Pestos, and Condiments

Fresh Tomato-Butter Sauce

*S*weet fresh tomatoes, cooked with a carrot and an onion in butter, become the perfect all-purpose sauce to serve on pasta, polenta, pizza, eggs, or vegetables.

Though I don't bother with a lot of kitchen gadgets, I do recommend investing in a food mill. Sure, a blender or food processor can puree a sauce, but the food mill goes one step further and separates the skins and seeds—which makes it unnecessary to peel and seed the tomatoes before cooking.

Makes about 3 cups

4 tablespoons (½ stick) unsalted butter

1 medium carrot, peeled and chopped

1 medium onion, chopped

4 pounds plum tomatoes, peeled and seeded, if not using a food mill, and chopped

Salt

6 fresh basil leaves, torn into bits

Melt the butter over medium heat in a large heavy saucepan. Add the carrot and onion and cook, stirring occasionally, until tender and golden, about 10 minutes. Add the tomatoes and a pinch of salt and cook, stirring often, until the tomatoes are soft and the sauce has thickened, about 30 minutes. Let cool slightly.

Pass the sauce through a food mill or puree it in a food processor or blender. Reheat gently and correct the seasoning.

Just before serving, stir in the basil.

Roasted Tomato Sauce

*W*hen summer comes and fresh tomatoes are at their best, I'm captivated by all the different kinds I find at my local farmers' market. I can't resist trying all of the heirloom varieties, from chocolate brown to striped green to sunny yellow. And I usually buy way too many: pear shape, round, big, and small. That's when I make this easy sauce by tossing them all together and roasting them until tender. The sauce is a little different every time, but it's always wonderful.

Toss with pasta, or slather on grilled bread for an easy appetizer.

Makes about 3 cups

2½ pounds mixed tomatoes, such as round, plum, grape, and cherry, chopped into ½-inch pieces
3 garlic cloves, finely chopped
Salt
Pinch of crushed red pepper
½ cup extra-virgin olive oil
½ cup shredded fresh basil

Preheat the oven to 400°F. Oil a 13-x-9-x-2-inch baking dish.

Toss the tomatoes, garlic, salt to taste, red pepper, and oil in the baking dish. Spread the tomatoes out evenly. Bake for 40 to 45 minutes, or until the tomatoes are lightly browned.

Just before serving, sprinkle the tomatoes with the basil and toss well.

Uncooked Tomato Sauce

*T*he height of summer, when tomatoes are their ripest, is the time to make this simple sauce, called *salsa crudaiola* in Italy. Serve it on pasta, toasted bread, grilled eggplant or mushrooms, hard-cooked eggs—the possibilities are endless.

Makes 2½ cups

2 large ripe tomatoes

10 fresh basil leaves, slivered

3 tablespoons extra-virgin olive oil

1 small garlic clove, finely chopped

Salt and freshly ground pepper

Cut the tomatoes in half lengthwise and remove the cores. Squeeze out the seeds. Chop the tomatoes and place in a bowl.

Add the basil, oil, garlic, and salt and pepper to taste to the tomatoes and stir well. (*The sauce can stand at room temperature for up to 1 hour.*)

VARIATIONS

• Add chopped arugula.

• Add ½ cup chopped pitted imported black olives, 2 or 3 anchovies, drained and minced, and 1 tablespoon chopped capers.

• Add a 5-ounce can of imported Italian tuna and a pinch of dried oregano.

• Add ½ cup chopped mixed fresh herbs, such as mint, parsley, thyme, and rosemary.

Spicy Onion Marmalade

When I received a jar of sweet onion marmalade as a gift, I wasn't quite sure what to do with it at first. It was dark purplish brown, and it was sweet, tart, and a little spicy. The label suggested it as a condiment for a sharp aged cheese. I loved it, and soon my husband and I were enjoying it with salami as an appetizer, as a dressing for panini, and on grilled cheese crostini.

Soon the jar was empty, I decided to make my own. This recipe is the result.

Makes about 1 cup

2 large red onions, quartered and thinly sliced

¼ cup water

½ teaspoon salt

¼ cup packed dark brown sugar

⅓ cup balsamic vinegar

Pinch of crushed red pepper

In a medium skillet, combine the onions, water, and salt, cover, and cook over medium-low heat for 15 minutes, or until the onions are softened.

Stir in the brown sugar and vinegar, cover, and cook, stirring occasionally, until the onions are very dark and soft and most of the liquid has evaporated, about 30 minutes. If the vinegar evaporates before the onions are cooked, add a spoonful of warm water. Once the onions are very tender, uncover and cook for a few minutes more, until most of the liquid has evaporated. Stir in the red pepper. Let cool.

Scrape the marmalade into an airtight container, cover, and refrigerate. (*The marmalade can be refrigerated for up to 1 month.*)

Cranberry-Fig Mostarda

*M*ostarda is a sweet and spicy condiment, similar to chutney, made from fruits flavored with mustard seeds. The tiny seeds add a tangy pop of flavor. For the famous *mostarda di Cremona*, a variety of fruits such as clementines, cherries, and figs are preserved in a clear syrup. One fruit I have never seen used in Italy is cranberries, which, with their sweet-tartness, seem to be an ideal choice. If they even exist there, they are certainly not very common.

With that in mind, I came up with this Italo-American mostarda made with cranberries and dried figs. It's wonderful at the holiday season with roast turkey, pork, or other meats. Or serve it with fresh goat cheese or some salami for an appetizer. It's the perfect dressing for those day-after-Thanksgiving turkey sandwiches. Packed into a pretty jar, it makes a nice gift.

Makes about 3½ cups

1 (12-ounce) bag cranberries, rinsed

7 ounces dried figs, stems removed and cut into ¼-inch pieces

1½ cups sugar

¼ cup orange juice

2 teaspoons yellow mustard seeds

1 tablespoon dry mustard, mixed with 1 tablespoon water

Combine the cranberries, figs, sugar, and orange juice in a large saucepan, bring to a simmer, cover, and cook, stirring occasionally, for 10 minutes, or until the cranberries pop.

Add the mustard seeds and mustard paste, stir well, and cook for 5 minutes more. Let cool.

Scrape the mostarda into an airtight container, cover, and refrigerate for 24 hours before serving. (*The mostarda can be refrigerated for at least 2 weeks.*)

Chunky Fig and Orange Jam

*H*omemade jam is a real treat, but I used to avoid it because I thought it would take hours and require special equipment. Then an Italian friend told me that the secret is making small batches.

This fig jam is a perfect example. It makes just one pint and can be stored in the refrigerator or freezer. It's a delight on toasted Italian bread with butter for breakfast or with bread and toasted walnuts in a cheese course.

Makes 1 pint

1 pound ripe figs, stemmed and quartered

1½ cups sugar

2 tablespoons fresh lemon juice

1 teaspoon grated orange zest

Place the figs in a saucepan with the sugar, lemon juice, and zest and cook over medium heat, stirring occasionally, until the juices begin to simmer. As the figs soften, crush them slightly with a potato masher or sturdy wire whisk. Continue to cook until the juices thicken slightly and are reduced, about 40 minutes.

To test the jam for doneness, drop some of the juice on a chilled plate and let cool slightly. Tilt the dish—the jam should run only slightly.

When the jam is ready, remove the saucepan from the heat and let cool.

Spoon the jam into jars or plastic freezer containers and cool completely, then cover and refrigerate for up to 2 weeks or freeze for up to 3 months.

Main Dishes

Broccoli Rabe
and Smoked Mozzarella Frittata

If you are accustomed to thinking of frittatas as mild-tasting and best suited to breakfast, this rendition might make you reconsider. The broccoli rabe and smoky cheese give this frittata a hearty flavor.

Serves 4

1 garlic clove, thinly sliced

3 tablespoons extra-virgin olive oil

2 cups bite-size pieces broccoli rabe

About 2 tablespoons water

8 large eggs

Salt and freshly ground pepper

4 ounces smoked mozzarella, sliced

Cook the garlic in the oil in a 10-inch nonstick skillet over medium heat until golden, about 1 minute. Add the broccoli rabe and the water. Cook, stirring, until the broccoli rabe is tender when pierced with a knife, about 8 minutes, adding a bit more water if it seems dry.

Whisk together the eggs and salt and pepper to taste in a bowl. Reduce the heat under the skillet to medium-low. Pour the egg mixture into the pan. Spread the broccoli rabe evenly in the pan and top with the mozzarella slices.

Cook, lifting the edges from time to time to allow the uncooked egg to reach the surface of the hot pan, until the frittata is partly set and lightly browned on the bottom, 8 to 10 minutes.

Slide the frittata onto a plate, brown side down, then invert the skillet over the plate and quickly flip the plate and skillet so that the brown side is up. Cook until just set in the center, about 5 minutes more. Or, if you prefer not to flip the frittata, use a flameproof skillet and slide it under a hot broiler for 3 to 5 minutes, or until the eggs are just set. (If the skillet has a plastic handle, wrap it in foil to protect it.)

Slide the frittata onto a serving dish and cut into wedges. Serve hot or at room temperature.

Sweet Pea Frittata
with Scallions and Ham

 frittata can be a great way to use leftover vegetables—or frozen ones. Peas and scallions give this one a subtle sweet flavor.

Serves 4

6 scallions, thinly sliced

3 tablespoons extra-virgin olive oil

1½ cups fresh or partially thawed frozen peas

½ cup chopped ham

8 large eggs

¼ cup chopped fresh parsley

¼ cup freshly grated Parmigiano-Reggiano

Salt and freshly ground pepper

In a 10-inch skillet, cook the scallions in the olive oil over medium heat until softened, about 2 minutes. Add the peas and ham and cook for 2 minutes more.

Meanwhile, whisk together the eggs, parsley, cheese, and salt and pepper to taste in a bowl.

Reduce the heat under the skillet to medium-low and pour the egg mixture into the pan. Cook, lifting the edges from time to time to allow the uncooked egg to reach the surface of the hot pan, until the frittata is partly set and lightly browned on the bottom, 8 to 10 minutes.

Slide the frittata onto a plate, brown side down, then invert the skillet over the plate and quickly flip the plate and skillet so that the brown side is up. Cook until just set in the center, about 5 minutes more. Or, if you prefer not to flip the frittata, use a flameproof skillet and slide it under a hot broiler for 3 to 5 minutes, or until the eggs are just set and the top is lightly browned. (If the skillet has a plastic handle, wrap it in foil to protect it.)

Slide the frittata onto a serving dish and cut into wedges. Serve hot or at room temperature.

Three-Cheese Eggplant Rollatini

"*S*wordfish and eggplant, eggplant and swordfish," I remember thinking the first time I visited Sicily many years ago. We seemed to be offered the same things at every meal. I was convinced that if Sicilians ate breakfast, they would probably eat swordfish and eggplant then too (actually, they prefer to eat gelato or granita).

There is a lot more variety in Sicilian cuisine today, but no one knows more ways to prepare eggplant than a Sicilian cook. These tasty little rolls never fail to please.

Serves 4

About ⅓ cup extra-virgin olive oil, plus more for brushing

1 large eggplant (about 1¼ pounds), trimmed and cut into ¼-inch-thick slices

Salt

1 cup whole-milk ricotta

¼ cup freshly grated Pecorino Romano

1 tablespoon shredded fresh basil

Freshly ground pepper

2 cups Marinara Sauce (page 171)

4 ounces mozzarella, cut into 2-x-½-x-½-inch sticks

Preheat the oven to 450°F. Oil two baking sheets. Brush the eggplant slices on both sides with the ⅓ cup oil, season with salt, and place them in a single layer on the baking sheets. Bake for 10 minutes, or until lightly browned on the bottom.

Turn the slices and bake for 5 to 10 minutes more, or until tender and lightly browned on the second side. Remove from the oven and let cool slightly. Reduce the oven heat to 350°F.

In a medium bowl, stir together the ricotta, 2 tablespoons of the Pecorino, the basil, and salt and pepper to taste.

Spread a thin layer of the sauce in a 9-x-9-x-2-inch baking dish. Place a spoonful of the ricotta mixture at one end of each eggplant slice. Lay a mozzarella stick across the end of each slice on top of the ricotta mixture. Roll up the eggplant slices and place seam side down in the baking dish. Spoon on the remaining sauce and sprinkle with the remaining 2 tablespoons Pecorino.

Bake the eggplant rolls for 25 to 30 minutes, or until the cheese is melted and the sauce is bubbling. Serve hot.

Eggplant Towers

Obikà, meaning "Here it is!" in Neapolitan dialect, is a small chain of casual restaurants, both in Italy and abroad, specializing in fresh mozzarella. Almost everything on the menu includes the cheese. At lunch in an Obikà in Rome, I had this fresh take on a classic combination of ingredients: eggplant, mozzarella, tomatoes, and basil.

Roasted eggplant slices are stacked with tomato and mozzarella, drizzled with a fresh-herb oil, and baked. To get the stacks even, try to find tomatoes that are as wide as the eggplant. The stacks can be assembled ahead of time and then baked when you are ready to serve them.

Serves 4

⅓ cup extra-virgin olive oil, plus more for brushing

2 medium eggplants (about 1 pound each), trimmed and cut into ½-inch-thick slices

Salt and freshly ground pepper

¼ cup fresh basil leaves

¼ cup fresh parsley leaves

2–3 large tomatoes, cut into eight ¼-inch-thick slices (total)

12 ounces mozzarella, cut into 8 slices

Preheat the oven to 425°F. Oil two large baking sheets with olive oil.

Brush the eggplant slices with olive oil on both sides. Arrange the slices in a single layer on the baking sheets. Sprinkle with salt and pepper to taste.

Bake for 10 to 15 minutes, or until lightly browned on the bottom. Flip the slices over and bake for 10 minutes more, or until browned on both sides and tender. Remove from the oven. You will need 8 slices for the towers; reserve the rest for sandwiches or another purpose. Reduce the oven heat to 375°F.

Meanwhile, pat the basil and parsley leaves dry with paper towels. Place them in a food processor or blender with a pinch of salt and chop fine. With the machine running, add the ⅓ cup olive oil and process until smooth. (*The basil oil can be made up to 4 hours ahead, covered, and refrigerated.*)

On a clean baking sheet, place 1 tomato slice on each of 4 of the eggplant slices. Sprinkle with salt and spread with a little of the basil oil. Place a cheese slice on top. Repeat with another layer of eggplant, season with salt and basil oil, and top with the remaining tomato slices and cheese. (If the stacks threaten to slide, stick a skewer or cocktail pick through the center to secure them.)

Bake the stacks for 15 minutes, or until the cheese is melting. Remove from the oven, drizzle with the remaining basil oil, and serve.

Romeo's Stuffed Eggplant

One of the first Italian cookbooks I bought when I was just married was penned by Romeo Salta, a chef who owned a restaurant in Manhattan that was very famous at that time. Mr. Salta, an immigrant from Puglia, in Southern Italy, had learned to cook while working on luxurious Italian ocean liners before coming to the United States, where he was employed in hotels and restaurants all around the country. Eventually he opened the restaurant in New York City that bore his name. It had a profound influence on Italian cooking in this country, and although it was one of the first restaurants to offer Northern Italian–style food here, Mr. Salta never forgot his Southern Italian roots.

This is one of the recipes that I learned from his book *The Pleasures of Italian Cooking.* I have adapted it somewhat.

Serves 4

Salt

2 medium eggplants (about 1 pound each), trimmed and halved lengthwise

1 large onion, chopped

¼ cup plus 2 tablespoons extra-virgin olive oil

1 cup chopped fresh or drained canned Italian tomatoes

½ teaspoon dried oregano

Freshly ground pepper

½ cup chopped pitted imported black olives

4 anchovy fillets, drained

3 tablespoons capers, rinsed and drained

¼ cup plain dry bread crumbs

¼ cup freshly grated Parmigiano-Reggiano

Bring a large pot of salted water to a boil. Oil a baking dish large enough to hold the eggplant halves.

Add the eggplant to the boiling water and cook for 5 minutes, or until softened. Drain and let cool.

Preheat the oven to 375°F.

Scoop out the eggplant flesh, leaving a ½-inch-thick shell. Place the eggplant shells side by side in the baking dish. Chop the flesh into ½-inch pieces.

In a large skillet, cook the onion in ¼ cup of the oil over medium heat until softened, about 8 minutes. Add the eggplant pieces, tomatoes, oregano, and salt and pepper to taste and cook for 10 minutes, or until the eggplant is tender. Stir in the olives, anchovies, capers, and bread crumbs.

Scrape the eggplant mixture into the shells. Sprinkle with the cheese. Drizzle with the remaining 2 tablespoons oil. Cover the baking dish with foil and bake for 35 minutes.

Remove the foil and bake for 15 minutes more, or until the eggplant is tender and the top is browned. Serve hot or at room temperature.

Sofia's Eggplant-Rice Timbale

I originally enjoyed this timbale while visiting the farm of my husband's cousin near Agrigento, in Southern Italy. Eggplant, tomato sauce, and cheese were layered with rice accented with golden saffron. The timbale was baked in the old wood-burning brick oven early in the day, and we ate it for lunch at a big table underneath the grape arbor.

Serves 8

Salt

Olive oil or vegetable oil for frying

2 medium eggplants (about 1 pound each), trimmed and cut into ¼-inch-thick slices

2 cups short-grain rice, such as Arborio

Pinch of saffron threads

Double recipe Marinara Sauce (page 171) (you will have 1 cup left over)

8 ounces imported Italian provolone or caciocavallo, thinly sliced

¼ cup freshly grated Parmigiano-Reggiano

Bring 5½ cups salted water to a boil in a large pot.

Meanwhile, in a large skillet, heat about ½ inch of oil until a small piece of eggplant sizzles when added to the skillet. Add only enough eggplant slices to make a single layer, without crowding, and fry, turning once, until nicely browned on each side, about 5 minutes. Remove with a slotted spoon and drain on paper towels. Fry the remaining slices in the same way.

Add the rice to the boiling water and crumble in the saffron. When the water returns to a boil, lower the heat, cover, and simmer for 15 to 18 minutes, or until the rice is tender and the water is absorbed. Remove from the heat.

Meanwhile, preheat the oven to 400°F. Oil a 13-x-9-x-2-inch baking dish.

Spread one third of the rice in the bottom of the baking dish. Top with half of the eggplant. Spread 1 cup of the sauce over the eggplant and top with one third of the provolone. Make a second layer, using half of the remaining rice, the remaining eggplant, 1 cup sauce, and half of the remaining provolone. Top with the remaining rice, sauce, and provolone. Sprinkle with the Parmesan.

Bake for 30 minutes, or until the timbale is bubbling and heated through. Let stand for 10 minutes before serving.

Stuffed Eggplant Balls

*R*omans call crispy little rice balls stuffed with mozzarella *supplì*, meaning "telephone wires," because of the way the cheese filling forms strings when the balls are cut open. These eggplant "balls" stuffed with cubes of smoked scamorza (you can use mozzarella instead) are inspired by *supplì*.

Serves 4

Salt

1 medium eggplant (about 1 pound), trimmed and cut lengthwise in half

1 large egg, beaten

1¼–1½ cups plain dry bread crumbs

¼ cup freshly grated Pecorino Romano

2 tablespoons chopped fresh parsley

Freshly ground pepper

3 ounces smoked scamorza or mozzarella, cut into ½-inch cubes

Olive oil or vegetable oil for frying

1 recipe Marinara Sauce (page 171), warmed

Bring a large pot of salted water to a boil. Add the eggplant halves to the boiling water, cover, and cook until tender when pierced with a knife, about 15 minutes. Place the eggplant halves cut side down in a colander and let cool completely.

Gently squeeze the eggplant to extract excess liquid. Chop it very fine (skin and all). Scrape it into a large bowl. Add the egg, ½ cup of the bread crumbs, the grated cheese, parsley, 1 teaspoon salt, and pepper to taste. Stir well; the mixture will be soft.

Make a test ball: Scoop up about 3 tablespoons of the mixture and shape it into a ball. If it is too soft, stir up to another ¼ cup bread crumbs into the eggplant mixture.

Spread the remaining ¾ cup bread crumbs on a plate. Shape 3 table-spoons of the eggplant mixture into a ball. Press a cube of scamorza into the center and mold the eggplant mixture around it to enclose it completely. Roll the ball in the crumbs, patting the crumbs on well, and place on a baking sheet. Repeat with the remaining mixture. Let the eggplant balls set up for about 15 minutes.

Preheat the oven to 200°F.

Pour about 2 inches of oil into a large heavy skillet and heat over medium heat until a pinch of the crumbs sizzles when dropped into the oil. Carefully place some of the balls in the pan, leaving a little space between them, and fry, turning occasionally, until evenly browned, about 10 minutes. Remove with a slotted spoon and drain on paper towels. Transfer to a baking sheet and keep warm in the oven while you fry the remainder.

Serve the eggplant balls with the tomato sauce.

Spicy Vegetable Stew

*D*uring the summer, I make this delicious stew all the time. It's good served with bread for a main course or piled on toast for an appetizer. You can also toss it with cooked pasta, eat it on a sandwich, or top it with a poached egg.

Serves 4 as a main dish
or 6 as an appetizer

1 medium onion, chopped

¼ cup extra-virgin olive oil

1 garlic clove, finely chopped

4 medium tomatoes, cut into bite-size pieces

3 medium waxy potatoes, such as Yukon Golds, peeled and cut into bite-size pieces

2 red bell peppers, cut into 1-inch squares

1 medium eggplant (about 1 pound), trimmed and cut into 1-inch chunks

Pinch of crushed red pepper

Salt

8 fresh basil leaves, torn into bits

In a large saucepan, cook the onion in the olive oil over medium heat until tender and golden, about 10 minutes. Stir in the garlic and cook for 1 minute. Add the tomatoes, potatoes, peppers, eggplant, red pepper, and salt to taste, cover, and cook, stirring occasionally, until the vegetables are tender and most of the liquid has evaporated, about 40 minutes. If the vegetables become too dry, add a little water. Or if there is too much liquid when the vegetables are tender, uncover the pan and cook until most of it is gone, about 5 minutes.

Sprinkle with the basil and serve hot or at room temperature.

Zucchini Parmesan

*A*s much as I love eggplant Parmesan, I think I like this Calabrian version with zucchini even more. It seems lighter and fresher, and the sharp caciocavallo cheese gives it a great flavor. If you can't find it, substitute an aged provolone—or, if you'd like a milder cheese flavor, use mozzarella.

Serves 6

⅓ cup unbleached all-purpose flour

½ teaspoon salt

Freshly ground pepper

Vegetable oil for frying

2½ pounds zucchini (about 6 medium), scrubbed, trimmed, and cut lengthwise into ¼-inch-thick slices

2 cups Marinara Sauce (page 171) or other plain tomato sauce

6 ounces caciocavallo, or aged imported Italian provolone, or mozzarella, sliced

6 fresh basil leaves, shredded

½ cup freshly grated Parmigiano-Reggiano or Pecorino Romano

On a plate, toss the flour with the salt and pepper to taste.

Heat about ½ inch of oil in a large skillet over medium heat until a bit of flour sizzles when sprinkled into the pan. Dip a few of the zucchini slices in the flour, tap off the excess, and carefully place the slices in the oil in a single layer, without crowding. Fry until golden brown on the first side, about 3 minutes. Turn the slices over and brown on the other side, 2 to 3 minutes more. Drain the slices on paper towels. Repeat with the remaining zucchini.

Preheat the oven to 350°F.

Spread a thin layer of the tomato sauce in a 9-x-9-x-2-inch baking dish. Place one third of the zucchini slices in the baking dish, overlapping them slightly. Break the cheese into small pieces and scatter half of them over the zucchini. Sprinkle with some of the basil. Top with another layer of sauce, half of the remaining basil, and a sprinkling of grated cheese. Repeat the layering using half of the remaining zucchini, the remaining cheese pieces, some sauce, and the remaining basil. End with a final layer of zucchini, sauce, and the remaining grated cheese. (*The dish can be made ahead to this point, covered, and refrigerated for up to 3 hours.*)

Bake for 45 minutes (longer if it's been refrigerated), or until the sauce is bubbling. Let stand for 10 minutes before serving. Serve hot.

Sausage-Stuffed Zucchini Boats

My mom used to make miniature eggplants stuffed with a meatball mixture. I was thinking about them one day and came up with this variation made with zucchini. Just a small amount of sausage adds big flavor to the stuffing. Pork sausage is my preference, but chicken or turkey are good too.

Serves 4

Salt

4 medium zucchini

1 medium onion, chopped

3 tablespoons extra-virgin olive oil

6 ounces sweet Italian pork sausage (about 2 links), casings removed

½ cup Rich Vegetable Broth (page 88) or chicken broth

1 medium tomato, halved, seeded, and chopped

Freshly ground pepper

⅓ cup plain dry bread crumbs

⅓ cup plus 2 tablespoons freshly grated Parmigiano-Reggiano

2 tablespoons chopped fresh parsley

1 large egg, beaten

Bring a large saucepan of salted water to a boil.

Trim the zucchini and cut in half lengthwise. With a small spoon, scoop out the pulp, leaving ½-inch-thick shells. Chop the pulp and set it aside.

Add the zucchini shells to the boiling water and cook for 3 minutes, or until just softened. Remove with tongs and place cut side down on paper towels to drain.

Preheat the oven to 400°F. Oil a 12-x-9-x-2-inch baking dish.

In a large skillet, cook the onion in the oil over medium heat until softened, about 5 minutes. Add the zucchini pulp and sausage and cook, stirring to break up the sausage, until the meat loses its pink color, about 5 minutes. Add the broth, tomato, and salt and pepper to taste and cook for 10 minutes, or until the liquid evaporates. Transfer to a bowl to cool.

Add the bread crumbs, ⅓ cup of the cheese, the parsley, and egg to the sausage mixture and stir well. Spoon the mixture into the zucchini shells and place the shells in the baking dish. Sprinkle the remaining 2 tablespoons cheese over the zucchini.

Bake for 25 to 30 minutes, or until the tops are lightly browned. Serve hot or at room temperature.

Pasta-Stuffed Peppers

Capers, olives, and anchovies are the Three Musketeers of Southern Italian cooking. Here they are mixed with tomatoes and pasta to stuff sweet bell peppers before roasting.

If the peppers are very large or if I am making these as part of an antipasto and want smaller portions, I cut the peppers in half lengthwise, scoop out the seeds, and stuff each half for smaller individual servings.

Serves 6

Salt

1 large garlic clove, finely chopped

2 tablespoons extra-virgin olive oil

3 large ripe tomatoes, chopped

½ teaspoon dried oregano

1 (2-ounce) can anchovy fillets, drained and chopped

2 tablespoons capers, rinsed and drained

¼ cup chopped pitted imported black olives

Freshly ground pepper

6 large red or yellow bell peppers

4 ounces ditalini, tubetti, or other small pasta

1 cup water

Preheat the oven to 375°F. Oil a baking dish just large enough to hold the peppers upright.

Bring a medium pot of salted water to a boil.

In a large skillet, cook the garlic in the oil over medium heat for 1 minute until softened. Stir in the tomatoes and oregano and cook, stirring occasionally, until most of the liquid has evaporated, about 5 minutes. Remove the pan from the heat and stir in the anchovies, capers, olives, and salt and pepper to taste.

Meanwhile, cut the tops off the peppers and set them aside. With a small sharp knife, remove and discard the seeds and the white membranes from the insides.

Add the pasta to the boiling water, stir, and cook, stirring frequently, until al dente. Drain well, then stir the pasta into the tomato sauce.

Fill each pepper about three-quarters full with the pasta mixture. Place the tops on them and arrange them in the baking dish. Pour the water around them.

Bake for 45 minutes, or until the peppers are tender when pierced with a fork. Serve warm.

Mozzarella-Stuffed Peppers

*L*ong, skinny sweet peppers are generally called Italian frying peppers, though I have also seen them sold as Cubanelle and banana peppers. Usually they are pale green in color, but in the summer I can often find locally grown red ones.

For additional flavor, add a little chopped prosciutto or pancetta to the stuffing. Serve these with a salad for a meal or as a side dish with barbecued pork or chicken.

Serves 6

6 large red or green Italian frying peppers (see headnote)

1 cup plain dry bread crumbs

1 garlic clove, grated (on a Microplane) or minced

½ cup freshly grated Pecorino Romano

¼ cup chopped fresh parsley

2 tablespoons chopped fresh oregano or ½ teaspoon dried

Salt and freshly ground pepper

¼ cup plus 2 tablespoons extra-virgin olive oil

4 ounces mozzarella, chopped

1 (28-ounce) can Italian crushed tomatoes

Preheat the oven to 425°F. Oil a 13-x-9-x-2-inch baking dish.

Cut the tops off the peppers and scoop out the seeds.

In a small bowl, stir together the bread crumbs, garlic, grated cheese, herbs, and salt and pepper to taste. Stir in ¼ cup of the olive oil until the crumbs are moistened. Stir in the mozzarella.

Spoon the stuffing into the peppers, tapping them to distribute the filling throughout. Arrange the peppers in the baking dish.

Stir together the crushed tomatoes and salt and pepper to taste. Pour the tomatoes over the peppers. Drizzle with the remaining 2 tablespoons oil.

Bake for 35 to 40 minutes, or until the peppers are tender and lightly browned. Serve warm.

Roman Rice-Stuffed Tomatoes with Roasted Potatoes

*B*ig sweet tomatoes stuffed with rice and roasted are a summer staple in Rome. The tomatoes get squishy soft and their flavor deepens. Sometimes wedges of potatoes are roasted alongside, and they soak up the herby tomato juices. Together the two make a satisfying meal.

Serves 6

Salt

²⁄₃ cup short-grain rice, such as Arborio

6 large ripe tomatoes

¼ cup plus 1 tablespoon extra-virgin olive oil

½ cup freshly grated Pecorino Romano

¼ cup chopped fresh basil or parsley

Freshly ground pepper

2 pounds waxy potatoes, such as Yukon Golds, peeled and cut into ½-inch-thick wedges

Bring 8 cups salted water to a boil in a medium saucepan. Add the rice and cook, uncovered, stirring occasionally, for 10 minutes. Drain and place the rice in a bowl.

Meanwhile, preheat the oven to 425°F.

Cut the top ½ inch off the tomatoes and reserve the caps. Scoop out the tomato pulp and juices. Chop the pulp and add it, with the juices, to the bowl with the rice. Add 2 tablespoons of the oil, the cheese, basil, and salt and pepper to taste. Stuff the mixture into the tomatoes and set the caps on top.

Put the potatoes in a baking pan large enough to hold them and the tomatoes in a single layer. Toss them with the remaining 3 tablespoons oil and salt to taste and spread them out. Bake for 15 to 20 minutes, or until just beginning to brown.

Toss the potatoes. Place the tomatoes in the pan between the potatoes.

Bake for 30 minutes more, or until the tomatoes and potatoes are tender.

Serve warm or at room temperature.

Easter Swiss Chard and Ricotta Pie

At Easter time, this savory tart is traditional in Liguria, but it has become so popular that you can now find it year-round. Some cooks make it with just one vegetable, while others use a mix like chard, spinach, arugula, beet greens, and/or artichoke hearts. Originally the tart was made with thirty-three layers of dough, representing the years of Jesus' life, but this is a streamlined contemporary version with just two layers enclosing the vegetable and cheese filling.

The crust for the pie is made with olive oil instead of butter or shortening, which gives it a melt-in-your mouth tenderness and great flavor. A vegan friend taught me a great trick: Freezing the oil to a slushy consistency makes the crust easier to handle.

Serves 8

Crust

½ cup extra-virgin olive oil

2½ cups unbleached all-purpose flour

1 teaspoon baking powder

1 teaspoon salt

About ¼ cup cold water

Filling

1 pound Swiss chard, stems removed

Salt

1 medium onion, finely chopped

2 tablespoons extra-virgin olive oil

2 large eggs

1 (15-ounce) container whole-milk ricotta

1 teaspoon chopped fresh marjoram or ½ teaspoon dried

Freshly ground pepper

¾ cup freshly grated Parmigiano-Reggiano

To make the crust

Place the olive oil in a small container in the freezer until it is slushy around the edges, 30 to 60 minutes.

In a food processor, pulse the flour, baking powder, and salt. (The dough can also be made with an electric mixer.) Add the olive oil and 2 tablespoons of the water and pulse to blend, adding the remaining water 1 tablespoon at a time as needed to make a smooth, soft dough. Remove the dough from the machine and cut it into 2 pieces, one twice as large as the other. Shape the pieces into disks. Wrap each piece in plastic wrap and refrigerate for at least 30 minutes, or overnight.

To make the filling

Bring a large pot of water to a boil. Add the Swiss chard and 2 teaspoons salt and cook for 7 to 10 minutes, until the chard is tender. Drain in a colander and cool under cold running water. Let cool completely.

Wrap the chard in a kitchen towel and squeeze well to extract as much liquid as possible. Place the chard on a cutting board and chop into ½-inch pieces.

In a medium skillet, cook the onion in the olive oil until tender and golden, about 10 minutes. Stir in the chard and cook for 5 minutes more. Remove from the heat and let cool.

continued on page 204

In a large bowl, whisk the eggs with the ricotta, marjoram, ½ teaspoon salt, and pepper to taste. Stir in the Parmigiano and the chard mixture until blended.

To assemble and bake

Preheat the oven to 350°F. Oil a 9-inch tart pan.

Roll out the larger piece of dough on a lightly floured surface to a 14-inch circle. Transfer the dough to the pan and fit it into the bottom and up against the sides. Trim off all but ½ inch of dough around the rim.

Scrape the filling into the pan.

Roll out the smaller disk of dough to a 10-inch circle and place it over the filling.

Roll the edge of the bottom crust up over the top and pinch together to seal. With a small knife, cut 6 small slits in the top crust to allow steam to escape.

Place the pan on a large baking sheet to catch any drips. Bake for 1 hour and 15 minutes, or until the pastry is browned. Cool the tart in the pan for 10 minutes.

Remove the rim of the pan and cut the tart into wedges. Serve warm or at room temperature.

Zucchini-Parmesan Torta

*C*heesy and eggy, with a moist, spongy, cake-like texture, this is good as a main dish or alongside a stew or roast. I've taken the somewhat unusual step of draining the grated zucchini and onion, and when you see how much liquid drips out, you will understand why it is worth the time to do it. Gruyère, Swiss, or Parmesan cheese is ideal here, but I've also made this with leftover chunks and scraps of whatever cheeses I have on hand, and it always tastes good.

Serves 6 as a main dish or 8 as a side dish

1 pound zucchini, scrubbed, trimmed, and grated (about 4 cups)

1 medium onion, grated (about ½ cup)

1 teaspoon salt

⅓ cup unbleached all-purpose flour

½ teaspoon baking powder

3 large eggs

¾ cup whole milk

1 cup grated Gruyère, Emmentaler, or Parmigiano-Reggiano

1 teaspoon chopped fresh marjoram or thyme

Place the zucchini and onion in a large strainer and toss them with the salt. Set the strainer over a bowl and let stand for 30 minutes.

Preheat the oven to 350°F. Butter and flour a 9-x-9-x-2-inch baking dish.

Place the drained vegetables in a kitchen towel and squeeze to remove the excess liquid. Discard the juices.

Stir together the flour and baking powder in a small bowl. In a large bowl, whisk the eggs and milk together. Whisk in the flour mixture in. Stir in the vegetables, cheese, and marjoram. Scrape the mixture into the baking dish.

Bake for 40 minutes, or until a knife inserted in the center comes out clean. Let cool for 10 minutes.

Cut the torta into squares and serve hot or at room temperature.

Spinach and Cheese Torta

You can think of this as a kind of baked frittata or savory cheesecake. Perfect for a main dish, brunch, or buffet, it unmolds beautifully. Any leftovers are great in a sandwich, perhaps with some sliced tomatoes.

I like to bake it in a springform pan, but be sure to slide the pan onto a baking sheet. Springforms can leak and make a smoky mess in the oven.

Serves 8 to 10

2 pounds spinach, washed and trimmed

¼ cup water

4 large eggs

1 teaspoon salt

Freshly ground pepper

⅛ teaspoon freshly grated nutmeg

1 (15-ounce) container whole-milk ricotta

1 cup plus 2 tablespoons freshly grated Parmigiano-Reggiano

Place the spinach in a large saucepan with the water, cover, and cook over medium heat for 5 to 10 minutes, or until just wilted. Drain well and let cool slightly.

Wrap the spinach in a kitchen towel and squeeze it to extract as much liquid as possible. Chop the spinach fine.

Preheat the oven to 350°F. Butter a 9-inch springform pan. Place the pan on a baking sheet.

In a large bowl, beat together the eggs, salt, pepper to taste, and nutmeg. Beat in the ricotta, the spinach, and 1 cup of the grated cheese until blended. Scrape the mixture into the pan. Smooth the top. Sprinkle with the remaining 2 tablespoons cheese.

Bake for 45 to 50 minutes, or until the torta is slightly puffed, set in the center, and lightly browned around the edges. Let cool for 10 minutes.

Run a knife around the inside of the pan rim and remove the rim. Cut the torta into wedges and serve hot or at room temperature.

Ricotta and Tomato Crostata

I had not planned to eat when I stopped for coffee at Gran Caffè La Caffettiera, a favorite café in Naples, but the assortment of *torte salate*, "savory tarts," looked too good to pass up. I settled on one made with ricotta and tomatoes. This is my version, baked in a free-form crust. Serve it for lunch or dinner or as an appetizer.

Serves 6 as a main dish
or 8 as an appetizer

Crust

1½ cups unbleached
all-purpose flour

¼ teaspoon salt

8 tablespoons (1 stick) cold
unsalted butter, cut into bits

1 large egg yolk

3–4 tablespoons ice water

Filling

1 cup whole-milk ricotta

¾ cup plus 2 tablespoons
freshly grated Parmigiano-
Reggiano

1 large egg

2 tablespoons shredded fresh
basil

Freshly ground pepper

3–4 medium tomatoes, thinly
sliced

To make the crust

In a food processor or large bowl, mix together the flour and salt. Add the butter and pulse or, if using a bowl, blend in with a pastry blender, until the mixture resembles coarse crumbs. Add the egg yolk and 3 tablespoons water and pulse or stir in with a fork until the mixture just begins to come together and form a ball. If it seems dry, add a little more water.

Scrape the dough onto a piece of plastic wrap and form it into a disk. Wrap tightly and refrigerate for at least 30 minutes or overnight.

Preheat the oven to 425°F.

To make the filling

In a bowl, whisk together the ricotta, ¾ cup of the grated cheese, the egg, basil, and pepper to taste.

To assemble and bake

On a lightly floured surface, roll out the dough to a 12-inch circle. Center the dough on a baking sheet. Spread the cheese mixture over the dough, leaving a 1-inch border all around. Arrange the tomato slices over the filling, overlapping them slightly. Sprinkle the remaining 2 tablespoons cheese over the tomatoes. Pleating it as you go, fold the border of dough over the filling.

Bake for 35 to 40 minutes, or until the pastry is golden brown and the filling is set. Cool the pan on a wire rack for 10 minutes.

Slide the crostata onto a serving platter and serve warm or at room temperature.

Side Dishes

Asparagus with Butter and Parmesan

*J*ust about any vegetable tastes great dressed with butter and Parmigiano-Reggiano, but asparagus is my favorite. This method is also good with green beans, carrots, broccoli, or zucchini.

Serves 4 to 6

Salt

1 pound asparagus, trimmed

2 tablespoons unsalted butter

Freshly ground pepper

⅓ cup freshly grated Parmigiano-Reggiano

Bring about 2 inches salted water to a boil in a large skillet. Add the asparagus and cook until the spears bend slightly when you lift them from the stem end, 4 to 8 minutes, depending on the thickness. Remove with tongs and pat dry.

Drain the skillet and wipe it dry. Add the butter and melt over low heat. Return the asparagus spears to the skillet and turn them briefly in the butter. Sprinkle with pepper to taste and the cheese. Cover the skillet, turn off the heat, and let stand for 1 minute, or until the cheese is melted. Serve.

VARIATIONS

Asparagus in Lemon Butter: Blanch the asparagus as directed above and pat dry. Melt the butter and add 1 tablespoon fresh lemon juice and a generous pinch of pepper. Turn the asparagus in the lemon butter until coated. Serve hot.

Asparagus with Balsamic Dressing: Blanch the asparagus as directed above and pat dry. In a shallow serving dish, whisk 3 tablespoons extra-virgin olive oil with 1 to 2 tablespoons balsamic vinegar (to taste) and salt and pepper to taste. Add the warm asparagus and turn in the dressing. Serve warm or chilled.

"Drowned" Broccoli

*W*hen I first read about this recipe, *broccoli affogati*, or "drowned broccoli," in an Italian cooking magazine, I thought it had too many ingredients and, because of the red wine, would look awful when done. The broccoli does lose its bright color, but the resulting dish is so good no one will care. The anchovies are traditional, but you can leave them out, if you like.

Serves 4 to 6

1 medium onion, chopped

3 tablespoons extra-virgin olive oil

1 garlic clove, chopped

1 large bunch broccoli (about 1¼ pounds), trimmed and cut into bite-size florets

6 anchovy fillets, drained and chopped (optional)

½ cup dry red wine

Salt

¼ cup shaved Pecorino Romano

In a large skillet, cook the onion in the oil over medium heat until tender and golden, about 8 minutes. Stir in the garlic and cook for 1 minute more. Add the broccoli, anchovies (if using), wine, and a pinch of salt, cover, reduce the heat to medium-low, and cook for 15 minutes, or until the broccoli is tender.

Sprinkle the broccoli with the cheese. Cover and let stand for 2 minutes, or until the cheese is melted. Serve.

Lemon-Roasted Broccoli

*R*ecently a friend was telling me how good her broccoli with lemon is. Rather than boiling or steaming it, she tosses it with lemon juice and roasts it, then sprinkles it with cheese. Now I have a new favorite way of cooking this vegetable.

Serves 6

1½ pounds broccoli, trimmed and cut into small florets

¼ cup extra-virgin olive oil

1–2 tablespoons fresh lemon juice

Salt and freshly ground pepper

⅓ cup freshly grated Pecorino Romano

Preheat the oven to 425°F.

In a baking pan large enough to hold the broccoli in a single layer, toss the florets with the oil, lemon juice, and salt and pepper to taste. Bake the broccoli for 15 minutes, or until lightly browned and almost tender.

Toss the broccoli, sprinkle with the cheese, and bake for 5 minutes more, or until the cheese is melted and the broccoli is tender. Serve.

Roasted Brussels Sprouts with Walnuts

*R*oasting brings out the nutty flavor of Brussels sprouts and turns them tender inside and crisp on the outside. For maximum flavor, be sure to roast them until they are dark brown.

Serves 8

1½ pounds Brussels sprouts, trimmed and halved through the base

2 ounces pancetta, finely chopped (optional)

3 tablespoons extra-virgin olive oil

Salt and freshly ground pepper

¼ cup coarsely chopped walnuts

Preheat the oven to 375°F.

In a baking pan large enough to hold all the Brussels sprouts in a single layer, toss the sprouts with the pancetta (if using), oil, and salt and pepper to taste. Roast for 35 minutes, or until the sprouts are deeply browned.

Add the walnuts and roast for 5 to 10 minutes more, or until the sprouts are tender and the nuts are toasted. Serve.

Baked Brussels Sprouts
with Butter and Parmesan

*T*he company recipes I like best are the ones I can prepare ahead of time
and finish when the guests arrive. This is one of them.
Asparagus, broccoli, fennel, and green beans can also be prepared this way.

Serves 6 to 8

Salt

1 pound Brussels sprouts,
trimmed and halved through
the base

2 tablespoons unsalted butter,
softened

Freshly ground pepper

½ cup freshly grated
Parmigiano-Reggiano

Bring a large saucepan of salted water to a boil. Add the Brussels sprouts and cook for 3 minutes, or until almost tender. Drain in a colander and cool under cold running water. Pat the sprouts dry. (*The sprouts can sit at room temperature for up to 2 hours.*)

Preheat the oven to 400°F. Coat a 9-x-9-x-2-inch baking dish with 1 tablespoon of the butter.

Add the sprouts to the baking dish and sprinkle with pepper to taste and the cheese. Dot with the remaining tablespoon of butter. Bake for 20 to 25 minutes, or until the sprouts are tender and the cheese is melted. Serve.

VARIATION

Baked Brussels Sprouts with Gorgonzola: Blanch the Brussels sprouts as above. Place them in the baking dish and sprinkle with 3 ounces crumbled Gorgonzola dolce. Dot with the butter and bake as directed.

Baked Balsamic Butternut Squash

*T*he tart sweetness of balsamic vinegar enhances the flavor of butternut and other winter squashes. This dish is good served hot with pork chops or sausages or at room temperature as an antipasto.

Serves 8

2 pounds butternut or acorn squash, halved lengthwise, seeded, peeled, and cut into ¼-inch-thick slices

3 tablespoons extra-virgin olive oil

Salt and freshly ground pepper

3 tablespoons balsamic vinegar

Preheat the oven to 400°F. Oil a 13-x-9-x-2-inch baking dish.

Toss the squash with the oil and salt and pepper to taste. Arrange the slices in the baking dish, overlapping them slightly. Cover with foil and bake for 40 minutes, or until tender.

Add the vinegar and toss the squash. Cook for 10 minutes more, or until the squash is glazed and the vinegar has evaporated.

Serve hot or at room temperature.

Tomato-Braised Cabbage

*C*hopped onion and tomatoes sweeten the flavor of the cabbage as they simmer together in the pan. For a spicier dish, add a pinch of crushed red pepper.

Serves 4 to 6

1 medium onion, finely chopped

¼ cup extra-virgin olive oil

1 small head green cabbage, cored and cut into bite-size pieces

1 (14- to 16-ounce) can chopped Italian tomatoes

¼ cup water

Salt and freshly ground pepper

In a large skillet, cook the onion in the oil over medium heat until tender and golden, about 8 minutes. Stir in the cabbage, tomatoes, water, and salt and pepper to taste, bring to a simmer, cover, and cook for 20 minutes, or until the cabbage is tender. If there is too much liquid, uncover and cook for 5 minutes more, until reduced.

Serve hot or at room temperature.

Baked Cardoons with Two Cheeses

A favorite spring and fall vegetable in Italy, cardoons are a mystery to most Americans. They resemble giant celery stalks but have a silvery green color. They taste like artichokes, which isn't surprising, because they are both members of the thistle family, but their meaty texture makes them much easier to eat.

The only difficult thing about cardoons may be finding them. You will need to locate a store with a good produce section.

The leaves are bitter and should be discarded. Cardoons must always be cooked before eating. Once they have been trimmed and boiled, they can be dressed with an oil and vinegar dressing, simmered in cream, added to soups, or fried. Here they are baked with two cheeses until hot and bubbly.

Serves 6

Salt

½ lemon

1 bunch cardoons (1¼ pounds)

Freshly ground pepper

4 ounces mild imported Italian provolone, Fontina Valle d'Aosta (see headnote page 54), or Gruyère, thinly sliced and cut into ½-inch-wide strips

2 tablespoons freshly grated Parmigiano-Reggiano

Bring a large saucepan of salted water to a boil.

Meanwhile, squeeze the lemon into a large bowl of cold water. Trim off the bottoms of the cardoons one at a time and cut away and discard any leaves. With a vegetable peeler or a paring knife, peel off the stringy outer layer of the stalks and any discolored portions. Cut the stalks into 3-inch lengths, dropping them into the lemon water as you go to prevent them from darkening.

Drain the cardoons and add them to the boiling water. Cook until tender when pierced with a knife, 15 to 30 minutes. Drain and let cool slightly.

Meanwhile, preheat the oven to 375°F. Butter a medium baking dish.

Arrange the cardoons in the dish, sprinkle with pepper to taste, and place the provolone on top. Sprinkle with the Parmesan.

Bake for 15 minutes, or until the cheese is melted. Serve.

Fried Cardoons

*I*n Piedmont, cardoons are served with bagna cauda (from the Italian *bagno caldo*, meaning "hot bath"), a dip made with butter, garlic, and anchovies. Neapolitan cooks use them in soup. Cardoons grow wild in some parts of California and are considered a nuisance by those who don't know how good they are to eat.

Crispy outside and creamy within, these sticks of fried cardoons make a fine appetizer or side dish. You can also prepare asparagus this way.

Serves 4 to 6

---

2 large eggs, beaten

Salt and freshly ground pepper

½ cup unbleached all-purpose flour

1 cup plain dry bread crumbs

½ bunch cardoons (about 10 ounces), prepared and boiled as on page 221

Olive or vegetable oil for frying

In a shallow bowl, beat the eggs with salt and pepper to taste. Spread the flour out on a small plate. Spread the bread crumbs out on another plate.

Roll the cardoons in the flour, dip them in the egg, and then roll them in the crumbs. Place the cardoons on a wire rack set over a baking sheet and let dry for at least 30 minutes. (*The cardoons can be prepared up to this point several hours ahead of time and refrigerated.*)

Heat about 1 inch of oil in a deep heavy saucepan over medium-high heat until the temperature reaches 370°F on a deep-fry thermometer; a bit of the bread crumbs should sizzle rapidly when dropped into the pan. Carefully add some of the cardoons to the oil; do not crowd the pan. Fry the pieces until nicely browned, turning once, about 4 minutes. Remove with a slotted spoon and drain on paper towels. Repeat with the remaining cardoons.

Sprinkle with salt and serve hot.

Carrots Cooked in Milk

A bit of milk brings out the sweetness of sliced carrots. The milk thickens slightly as the carrots simmer and forms soft, creamy curds. My friend Cecilia Martorella, whose family came from Milan, told me that her mother always cooked carrots this way. For kids who are skeptical about eating vegetables, this preparation is an ideal choice.

Serves 4

1 pound carrots, peeled and thinly sliced

¾ cup whole milk

1 tablespoon unsalted butter

½ teaspoon sugar

⅛ teaspoon freshly grated nutmeg

Pinch of salt

Combine all the ingredients in a large nonstick skillet, bring to a simmer, and cook, stirring occasionally, until most of the milk evaporates and the carrots are tender, about 15 minutes.

Taste for seasoning and serve.

Roasted Cauliflower
with Spicy Bread Crumbs

*T*oasty and garlicky, these bread crumbs are so good I could eat them with a spoon. But that would deprive the cauliflower of their great flavor. You will find that the crumbs complement many other vegetables. Try them on roasted sliced peppers or cooked green beans or broccoli. You can also toss the cauliflower and crumbs with pasta and some of the pasta cooking water to make a sauce.

Serves 6 to 8

1 large head cauliflower (about 2 pounds), trimmed and cut into bite-size florets

¼ cup extra-virgin olive oil

Salt

¼ cup plain dry bread crumbs

1 small garlic clove, finely chopped

Pinch of crushed red pepper

2 tablespoons finely chopped fresh parsley

Preheat the oven to 425°F.

On a large baking sheet, toss the cauliflower with 3 tablespoons of the oil and salt to taste. Roast, turning the cauliflower at least twice, for 20 to 30 minutes, until nicely browned.

Meanwhile, heat the remaining 1 tablespoon oil in a small skillet. Add the bread crumbs, garlic, a pinch of salt, and the red pepper and cook, stirring often, until the crumbs are crisp and browned, 4 to 5 minutes. Remove from the heat.

Sprinkle the cauliflower with the crumbs and parsley and toss well. Serve.

Roasted Cauliflower
with Raisins and Capers

*R*oasting lightly crisps and caramelizes the cauliflower, which gets a boost of sweetness from raisins and balsamic vinegar and a salty tang from capers. Serve this as a side dish with fish fillets or as part of an antipasti or vegetable buffet.

Serves 6

1 medium head cauliflower (about 1½ pounds), trimmed and cut into small florets

1 medium red onion, cut into 8 wedges

¼ cup extra-virgin olive oil

Salt and freshly ground pepper

¼ cup golden raisins

2 tablespoons capers, rinsed and drained

2 tablespoons balsamic vinegar

Preheat the oven to 425°F.

In a large roasting pan, toss together the cauliflower, onion, oil, and salt and pepper to taste. Roast, turning the vegetables at least twice, for 20 to 30 minutes, until they are nicely browned.

While the cauliflower is roasting, soak the raisins in warm water to cover until plumped. Drain.

Add the raisins and capers to the cauliflower and cook for 5 minutes more. Drizzle with the balsamic vinegar and toss.

Serve hot or at room temperature.

Glazed Roasted Eggplant

*B*alsamic vinegar is a great ingredient for enhancing the flavor of many vegetables. Here it works its magic on eggplants, creating a slightly sweet glaze.

Serves 6 to 8

3 tablespoons extra-virgin olive oil

2 tablespoons balsamic vinegar

½ teaspoon salt

Freshly ground pepper

8 miniature eggplants (about 1½ pounds), such as Japanese or Fairytale, trimmed and cut lengthwise in half

Preheat the oven to 400°F.

In a 13-x-9-x-2-inch baking dish, whisk together the oil, vinegar, salt, and pepper to taste. Add the eggplant halves and turn them to coat. Arrange the eggplants cut side down in the dish in a single layer.

Bake for 25 to 30 minutes, or until the cut sides are browned and the eggplants are tender. Check the pan after 20 minutes to be sure that the dressing has not completely dried up; if it has, add a spoonful of water to the dish.

Serve warm.

Summertime Eggplant

*S*callions complement the light cherry tomato sauce on these roasted eggplant slices. I sometimes make a meal of this with some crusty bread and Pecorino cheese.

Serves 4

1 large eggplant (about 1¼ pounds), trimmed and cut into ¼-inch-thick slices

2 tablespoons extra-virgin olive oil, plus more for brushing

Salt

4 scallions, chopped

1 pint cherry or grape tomatoes, halved, juice reserved, or one 14-ounce can imported Italian cherry tomatoes, with their juice

4 fresh basil leaves, torn into bits

2 tablespoons freshly grated Pecorino Romano

Preheat the oven to 450°F.

Brush the eggplant slices with olive oil on both sides. Place the slices in a single layer on a baking sheet. Sprinkle lightly with salt.

Bake the eggplant for 15 minutes, or until lightly browned on the bottom. Turn the slices and bake for 5 minutes more, or until tender and cooked through.

Meanwhile, cook the scallions in the 2 tablespoons oil in a medium saucepan over medium heat, stirring occasionally, until softened, about 3 minutes. Add the tomatoes, with their juice, and a pinch of salt and cook for 15 to 20 minutes for fresh (less for canned), mashing the tomatoes with the back of a spoon, until the sauce has thickened. Stir in the basil and remove from the heat.

Arrange the eggplant slices on a platter. Spoon on the sauce, sprinkle with the cheese, and serve.

Naples-Style Eggplant Cutlets

*E*ggplant slices are typically dipped in egg, cheese, and bread crumbs before frying. Hard to resist, but on the heavy side. On a visit to Naples, I learned this lighter method for frying them. Without the crumbs or cheese, the flavor of the vegetable shines through.

Serve the cutlets hot or at room temperature. I like them as is, but they are also good with a tomato sauce. They are great in sandwiches too.

Serves 4 to 6

1 large eggplant (about 1¼ pounds), trimmed and cut into ¼-inch-thick slices

Salt

2 large eggs

Freshly ground pepper

1 cup unbleached all-purpose flour

Olive or vegetable oil for frying

Sprinkle the eggplant slices on both sides with salt.

In a shallow bowl, beat the eggs with salt and pepper to taste. Spread the flour on a plate.

Heat about ½ inch of oil in a large skillet over medium-high heat until hot; a bit of the eggs dropped into the oil should sizzle rapidly.

Quickly dip an eggplant slice into the eggs, then into the flour, tapping off the excess, and carefully place in the oil. Continue with additional slices, making a single layer in the pan. (Coating the slices just before frying ensures that the crust comes out crisp.) Fry the eggplant for 3 to 4 minutes, or until nicely browned. With tongs, turn the slices over and fry on the second side, about 2 minutes more. Drain on paper towels.

Repeat with the remaining eggplant.

Sprinkle the eggplant with salt and serve hot or at room temperature.

Cipollini Agrodolce

*M*ellow little onions roasted in the sweet and tangy glaze known as *agrodolce* are a perfect accompaniment to pork ribs or chops or a frittata, or serve as part of an antipasti assortment.

Either white or red cipollini can be used, or substitute pearl onions.

Serves 6 to 8

1 pound cipollini or pearl onions, unpeeled

1 tablespoon chopped fresh rosemary

Salt and freshly ground pepper

¼ cup balsamic vinegar

2 tablespoons extra-virgin olive oil

1 tablespoon honey

Bring a large saucepan of water to a boil. Add the onions and cook for 1 minute after the water returns to a boil. Drain in a colander and cool under cold running water.

Preheat the oven to 425°F.

With a small paring knife, shave off the root end of each onion and slip off the skins. Place the onions in a baking pan just large enough to hold them in a single layer. Add the rosemary, salt and pepper to taste, vinegar, oil, and honey and toss well.

Bake, stirring occasionally, until the onions are tender and glazed with the pan juices, 20 to 30 minutes. If the pan becomes too dry before the onions are done, add a tablespoon or two of warm water.

Serve warm or at room temperature.

Roasted Fennel and Potatoes with Garlic

*E*very time I prepare this, I wish I had made more. Everybody loves it, and it disappears fast. Make sure you use a large enough pan so that all the fennel and potatoes brown nicely. A 17-x-12-x-1-inch baking sheet does the trick.

Serves 4

1 large fennel bulb, trimmed

3 tablespoons extra-virgin olive oil

1 pound waxy potatoes, such as Yukon Golds, sliced ¼ inch thick

Salt and freshly ground pepper

1 large garlic clove, minced

Preheat the oven to 425°F.

Cut the fennel through the core into ½-inch-thick wedges. (Leaving the core attached helps the slices keep their shape.)

Brush a 17-x-12-x-1-inch baking sheet with 1½ tablespoons of the oil. Add the fennel and potato slices in a single layer. Brush the top sides with the remaining 1½ tablespoons oil. Sprinkle with salt and pepper to taste.

Roast the vegetables for 20 minutes, or until browned. Flip them and sprinkle with the garlic and additional salt and pepper to taste. Bake for 10 minutes more, or until they are tender and browned.

Serve hot or at room temperature.

Golden Braised Fennel

*B*raised fennel is good with seafood, pork, or chicken. A small amount of water along with the butter in the pan allows the fennel to turn meltingly soft and tender.

Serves 6

2 medium fennel bulbs, trimmed

3 tablespoons unsalted butter

½ cup water

Salt and freshly ground pepper

¼ cup freshly grated Parmigiano-Reggiano

Cut the fennel through the core into ½-inch-thick wedges. (Leaving the core attached helps the slices keep their shape.)

Melt the butter in a 10-inch skillet over medium heat. Pat the fennel wedges dry and place them in the skillet in a single layer. Cook until they begin to brown, about 4 minutes. Turn and brown on the second side.

Add the water and sprinkle the fennel with salt and pepper to taste. Bring to a simmer, then cover the pan, turn the heat to low, and cook until the fennel is tender, about 20 minutes. If it becomes too dry, add a little more water.

Sprinkle the fennel with the cheese, cover the pan, and cook for 1 minute more, or until the cheese has melted. Serve.

Creamy Fennel Gratin

When I was a child, we often ate fennel, but it was always served raw. Crunchy and refreshing, it appeared with a big bowl of assorted fruit after a meal. My father always said it was good for the digestion. Later I learned that he was right. Fennel is also high in antioxidants and vitamin C.

When cooked, fennel turns soft and yielding and its mellow anise flavor is enhanced. This is one of my favorite ways to eat it.

Serves 6 to 8

Salt

2 large fennel bulbs, trimmed and cut into ½-inch-thick wedges

2 tablespoons unsalted butter, cut into bits

½ cup heavy cream

Freshly ground pepper

½ cup freshly grated Parmigiano-Reggiano

Preheat the oven to 400°F. Butter a 13-x-9-x-2-inch baking dish.

Bring a large saucepan of salted water to a boil. Add the fennel and cook for 5 minutes, or until almost tender. Drain in a colander and cool slightly under cold running water. Drain well and pat dry.

Place the fennel wedges in the baking dish, overlapping them slightly. Dot with the butter and drizzle with the cream. Sprinkle with pepper to taste and the cheese.

Bake for 15 to 20 minutes, or until browned and bubbly. Serve.

Green Beans with Garlic and Anchovies

*G*arlic and anchovies elevate plain green beans to nothing short of fantastic. The beans can be boiled ahead of time, but do not refrigerate them or they will lose their fresh flavor.

If you prefer to leave out the anchovies, add a tablespoon or two of chopped capers or olives to amp up the flavor.

Serves 6

Salt

1 pound thin green beans, trimmed

2 tablespoons unsalted butter

2 tablespoons extra-virgin olive oil

1 garlic clove, finely chopped

6 anchovy fillets, drained and chopped (see headnote)

Freshly ground pepper

2 tablespoons chopped fresh parsley

Bring a large saucepan of salted water to a boil. Add the green beans and cook until crisp-tender, about 7 minutes. Drain in a colander and cool under cold running water; drain well. (*The beans can be boiled up to 3 hours ahead, wrapped in a paper towel, and left at room temperature.*)

Wipe the saucepan dry. Add the butter and oil and melt the butter over medium heat. Add the garlic and anchovies and cook, mashing the anchovies with the back of a spoon, for about 2 minutes, until they dissolve. Add the green beans and salt and pepper to taste and cook, tossing well, for about 1 minute.

Add the parsley, toss again, and serve.

Green Beans with Pancetta, Red Onions, and Parsley

*P*ancetta is made from the same cut of pork as bacon. The meat is salted and seasoned with black pepper and garlic. Then it is rolled up and pressed into a log to be aged and cured. Sometimes pancetta is smoked like bacon, but usually it is not. Along with red onion, it adds great flavor to green beans.

These beans are great on their own or folded into beaten eggs for a frittata.

Serves 4

Salt

1 pound green beans, trimmed

2 ounces pancetta, cut into thin slivers

2 tablespoons extra-virgin olive oil

1 large red onion, halved and thinly sliced

Freshly ground pepper

1 tablespoon chopped fresh parsley

Bring a large pot of salted water to a boil. Add the beans and cook until almost but not quite tender, about 7 minutes. Drain in a colander and cool under cold running water; drain well.

In a large skillet, cook the pancetta in the olive oil for 5 minutes, or until lightly browned. Add the onion and cook for 8 minutes, stirring occasionally, until tender. Stir in the green beans and salt and pepper to taste and cook, stirring, until the beans are tender, about 2 minutes more.

Sprinkle with the parsley and serve.

Sautéed Mushrooms
with Garlic and Parsley

*B*rowned, garlicky mushrooms are good as a side dish, folded into an omelet, or piled on top of polenta, pasta, crostini, or a steak. For a spicy touch, add a pinch of crushed red pepper along with the oil. In Italy, these are called *funghi trifolati*, "truffle-style mushrooms," because of their intense, truffle-like flavor.

Serves 4

¼ cup extra-virgin olive oil

1 (10- to 12-ounce) package button or cremini mushrooms, cleaned, trimmed, and sliced

Salt and freshly ground pepper

2 large garlic cloves, thinly sliced

2 tablespoons chopped fresh parsley

In a large skillet, heat the oil over medium heat. Add the mushrooms and salt and pepper to taste and cook, stirring often, until the mushrooms release their liquid, about 5 minutes. Stir in the garlic and cook until the mushrooms are tender and browned, about 8 minutes more.

Stir in the parsley and serve.

VARIATION

Stir in 1 or 2 chopped tomatoes and a pinch of crushed red pepper along with the garlic.

Sweet Peas with Tomato and Onion

*S*weet peas have such a brief season that I rely on frozen most of the year. This recipe makes the most of them by adding sautéed onion and tomato. If you have some fresh basil, sprinkle it in at the end of the cooking.

Serves 4

1 small onion, finely chopped

2 tablespoons extra-virgin olive oil

½ cup chopped fresh or canned Italian tomatoes

Salt and freshly ground pepper

1 (10-ounce) package frozen peas

¼ cup water

In a medium skillet, cook the onion in the oil over medium heat until tender and golden, about 10 minutes. Add the tomato and salt and pepper to taste and cook for 5 minutes, or until the tomato is softened.

Add the peas and water, cover, reduce the heat to low, and cook for 5 minutes, or until the peas are tender. Serve.

VARIATION

To turn the peas into a speedy one-dish meal, crack some eggs and place on top of the cooked peas, sprinkle some grated cheese over the peas, clamp a lid on the pan, and cook until the eggs are done to taste.

Crusty Roasted Peppers

*S*trips of tender bell peppers are roasted with crunchy, savory bread crumbs. If you like, add some grated cheese to the crumb mixture. These peppers are nice with grilled tuna or swordfish.

Serves 6

2 large red bell peppers, cut into ½-inch-wide strips

2 large yellow bell peppers, cut into ½-inch-wide strips

Salt and freshly ground pepper

¼ cup extra-virgin olive oil

⅓ cup plain dry bread crumbs

1 large garlic clove, minced

2 tablespoons capers, rinsed and drained

2 tablespoons chopped fresh parsley

Preheat the oven to 375°F.

In a 13-x-9-x-2-inch baking dish, toss the peppers with salt and pepper to taste and 2 tablespoons of the olive oil. Spread the peppers out evenly in the dish. Bake for 20 minutes, or until the peppers are beginning to brown.

Toss the bread crumbs with the remaining 2 tablespoons oil, the garlic, capers, and parsley. Sprinkle the crumbs over the peppers and stir well. Bake for 15 minutes more, or until the peppers are tender and the crumbs are browned.

Serve hot or at room temperature.

Tomato Mashed Potatoes

I thought I had tried just about every mashed potato variation there was until I tasted this one at a Roman trattoria. The cooked potatoes are mashed and mixed with a lightly spiced tomato sauce for both flavor and color.

You can serve them as is, but for a dramatic presentation, do as they do in Rome and pack them into an oiled bowl to give them a neat shape. Then invert onto a serving platter and cut into wedges. Simple enough for a family meal, these potatoes are also a pretty accompaniment to a holiday dinner.

Serves 6

1½ pounds waxy potatoes, such as Yukon Golds, scrubbed

1 small onion, finely chopped

Pinch of crushed red pepper

¼ cup extra-virgin olive oil

2 cups tomato puree

Salt and freshly ground pepper

Place the potatoes in a large saucepan with cold water to cover, cover, and bring to a boil. Reduce the heat and simmer for 20 to 25 minutes, or until the potatoes are tender when pierced with a knife. Drain and let cool slightly.

Meanwhile, in a large saucepan, cook the onion and red pepper in the olive oil over medium heat for 10 minutes, or until the onion is golden. Add the tomato puree and cook for 15 minutes, or until the sauce is slightly thickened.

Peel the potatoes and place them in a bowl. Mash them with a potato masher or wire whisk until smooth.

Stir the potatoes into the sauce just until blended. Season to taste with salt and pepper and serve.

Lemon Potatoes

*P*otatoes, lemon, and rosemary bake together, their flavors marrying in this ideal dish to serve with fish.

The secret to cooking the potatoes is to spread them out in the pan so that they brown nicely. But watch them carefully, for if your pan is thin, the lemon slices may burn before the potatoes are done. If they darken too quickly, lower the oven temperature by 25 degrees.

Serves 6

3 lemons

1¼ pounds waxy potatoes, such as Yukon Golds, scrubbed and cut into ¼-inch-thick slices

3 tablespoons extra-virgin olive oil

1 tablespoon chopped fresh rosemary

1 teaspoon salt

Freshly ground pepper

Preheat the oven to 375°F. Oil a 17-x-12-x-1-inch baking sheet.

Cut one of the lemons in half and squeeze to obtain 2 tablespoons juice.

Trim the ends off the remaining 2 lemons and cut the lemons into thin, even slices. Remove the seeds. Scatter the slices over the pan.

In a large bowl, toss the potatoes with the olive oil, lemon juice, rosemary, salt, and pepper to taste. Scrape the potatoes onto the pan, spreading them out into a single layer.

Bake for 25 minutes, or until the potatoes are just beginning to brown.

Turn the potatoes and lemons and bake for 15 to 20 minutes more, or until browned and crisp. Serve.

Potato and Mushroom Gratin

When I first had this dish in Piedmont, it was made with earthy porcini mushrooms. Since they are hard to find here, I substitute a mix of cultivated varieties, such as shiitake, cremini, and white.

The sautéed mushrooms are mixed with cream and milk to form a sauce for the potato slices. I like to serve this luscious casserole as a side dish for a roast, but with its sprinkling of cheese, it is rich enough to be a main dish with a salad.

Serves 8

2 tablespoons unsalted butter

8 ounces shiitake mushrooms, cleaned, stems discarded, and sliced

8 ounces cremini or white mushrooms, cleaned, trimmed, and sliced

1 garlic clove, minced

Salt and freshly ground pepper

1 cup heavy cream

½ cup whole milk

2½ pounds waxy potatoes, such as Yukon Golds, peeled and cut into ⅛-inch-thick slices

½ cup freshly grated Parmigiano-Reggiano

Preheat the oven to 375°F. Butter a 13-x-9-x-2-inch baking dish.

Melt the butter in a large skillet over medium heat. Add the mushrooms and cook, stirring often, until the liquid they release evaporates, about 5 minutes. Add the garlic and salt and pepper to taste and cook for 5 minutes, or until the mushrooms are golden. Stir in the cream and milk and bring to a simmer. Remove from the heat.

Spread one third of the potato slices in the baking dish. Sprinkle lightly with salt. Add half of the mushrooms and liquid. Make a second layer with half of the remaining potatoes, season with salt, and top with the remaining mushrooms and liquid. Arrange the remaining potatoes on top and sprinkle them with salt and pepper to taste. Sprinkle with the cheese.

Bake the gratin for 45 to 60 minutes, until the potatoes are tender and the top is browned. Let rest for 5 minutes before serving.

Zucchini and Pepper Skillet

*T*his stir-fry makes the most of zucchini and bell peppers, two of summer's most prolific vegetables. It's good as a side dish, over pasta, in an omelet, or in a sandwich, topped with cheese. If you have some fresh basil or parsley, chop it and add it at the end.

Serves 6 to 8

1 medium onion, thinly sliced

2 medium red bell peppers, sliced into strips

¼ cup extra-virgin olive oil

1 pound small to medium zucchini, scrubbed, trimmed, and thinly sliced

Salt and freshly ground pepper

In a large skillet, cook the onion and bell peppers in the oil over medium heat, stirring occasionally, for 10 minutes, or until softened but not browned.

Add the zucchini and salt and pepper to taste and cook over medium-low heat, stirring occasionally, for 10 minutes, or until the vegetables are tender.

Serve hot or at room temperature.

Grilled Vegetables with Herb Dressing

*H*ere is a basic recipe for grilling vegetables outdoors on a grill or indoors on the stovetop. I use this method all the time with different vegetables as they come into season. Other choices include scallions, asparagus, bell pepper wedges, fennel, and radicchio.

The grilled vegetables are good in sandwiches and omelets or tossed with pasta.

Serves 6

About ½ cup extra-virgin olive oil

1 garlic clove, minced

2 tablespoons chopped fresh parsley

½ teaspoon chopped fresh thyme

Salt and freshly ground pepper

1 medium eggplant, trimmed and cut into ½-inch-thick slices

2 small to medium zucchini, scrubbed, trimmed, and cut into ¼-inch-thick diagonal slices

1 large red onion, cut into ½-inch-thick slices

Preheat a barbecue or stovetop grill until very hot.

In a small bowl, stir together ¼ cup of the oil, the garlic, parsley, thyme, and salt and pepper to taste. Set aside.

Brush the vegetables on both sides with the remaining ¼ cup olive oil. Grill (in batches on the stovetop) until browned on the first side, about 5 minutes. Turn the slices and cook until browned on the second side and tender, about 5 minutes more.

Arrange the eggplant and zucchini on a platter, overlapping slightly. Separate the onion into rings and scatter them over the eggplant and zucchini. Drizzle with the dressing.

Serve hot or at room temperature.

Spinach (or Other Greens) with Garlic and Hot Pepper

*A*ll kinds of greens are good cooked this way. Try Swiss chard, escarole, dandelion greens, arugula, or beet greens. For firmer vegetables like broccoli, broccoli rabe, kale, and collards, add a little bit of water to prevent them from scorching. You can serve these with practically anything, use them as a topping for pizza and crostini, or toss them with pasta or cooked dried beans for an easy main course.

Serves 4

3 garlic cloves, thinly sliced

Pinch of crushed red pepper (optional)

¼ cup extra-virgin olive oil

1½ pounds spinach, washed, drained well, and trimmed

Salt

In a large saucepan, cook the garlic and red pepper, if using, in the oil over medium heat until the garlic is golden, about 2 minutes. Add the spinach and sprinkle it with salt. (Be careful, because the hot oil can sputter and splash if the vegetables are wet. If cooking firmer vegetables, add ¼ cup water.)

Cover the pan and cook, stirring once or twice, until the spinach is tender and wilted, about 4 minutes (longer for firmer vegetables). Serve hot or at room temperature.

VARIATIONS

• Use butter instead of oil.

• Sprinkle the cooked greens with a dash of fresh lemon juice or vinegar.

• Sprinkle with grated Parmesan cheese.

Swiss Chard with Tomato and Garlic

o eliminate the excess liquid and tenderize the Swiss chard, I blanch it first and press out the liquid. Escarole is also good cooked this way.

Serves 6

Salt

1 large bunch Swiss chard (about 1½ pounds), washed and cut into ½-inch-wide strips

2 medium tomatoes or 1 cup canned Italian tomatoes

2 large garlic cloves, thinly sliced

3 tablespoons extra-virgin olive oil

Freshly ground pepper

Bring a large saucepan of salted water to a boil. Add the Swiss chard, bring the water back to a boil, and cook for 5 minutes, or until wilted. Drain well in a colander or strainer and let cool, then press out the excess liquid.

If using fresh tomatoes, cut them in half and squeeze the halves to extract the seeds. If using canned, drain them slightly. Chop the tomatoes.

In a large skillet, cook the garlic in the oil over medium heat for 1 minute, or until golden. Add the tomatoes and salt and pepper to taste, then add the chard and mix well. Cook for 10 minutes, or until the chard is tender. Serve.

Swiss Chard with Raisins and Pine Nuts

 nion, garlic, raisins, and pine nuts give Swiss chard a great flavor. Serve it with cooked dried beans such as cannellini for an easy meatless meal.

Serves 6

1 medium onion, chopped

2 tablespoons extra-virgin olive oil

2 garlic cloves, finely chopped

½ cup raisins

1 large bunch Swiss chard (about 1½ pounds), washed and cut into ½-inch-wide strips

Salt and freshly ground pepper

¼ cup pine nuts, lightly toasted

In a large saucepan, cook the onion in the oil over medium heat, stirring often, until softened, about 5 minutes. Stir in the garlic and raisins, add the Swiss chard and salt and pepper to taste, and stir well. Cover and cook until the chard is wilted, about 10 minutes.

Uncover and cook until most of the liquid evaporates. Sprinkle with the pine nuts and serve.

Utica Greens (Spicy Escarole)

These cheesy, spicy greens are a local favorite in restaurants and home kitchens in Utica, New York, home to a large Italian-American population. There are many variations, some with fried potatoes or sausage chunks added, or Swiss chard, spinach, kale, or broccoli rabe instead of the escarole. The greens are so beloved that each year the Utica Music and Arts Fest invites different restaurants to the music festival to serve their special versions.

You can also serve these as an appetizer with hunks of crusty bread or in a sandwich with grilled sausages or breaded veal cutlets.

Serves 4 to 6

Salt

1½ pounds escarole, washed and trimmed

2 garlic cloves, thinly sliced

2 ounces sliced prosciutto (about 4 slices), chopped

¼ cup extra-virgin olive oil

4–5 pickled hot cherry peppers or peperoncini, seeded and chopped

Freshly ground pepper

2 tablespoons plain dry bread crumbs

½ cup freshly grated Pecorino Romano

Bring a large saucepan of salted water to a boil. Add the escarole, return the water to a boil, and cook for 5 minutes, or until wilted. Drain well.

In a large ovenproof skillet, cook the garlic and prosciutto in the oil over medium heat until the prosciutto is golden, about 3 minutes. Add the escarole, pickled peppers, and pepper to taste and cook, stirring, for 2 minutes, or until thoroughly mixed. Remove from the heat and spread the mixture out evenly in the pan.

Place the broiler rack about 3 inches away from the heat and turn on the broiler.

Toss together the bread crumbs and cheese and sprinkle over the greens. Place the skillet under the broiler for 4 to 5 minutes, or until the topping is golden. Serve.

Salads

Peach, Tomato, and Burrata Salad

$\mathcal{I}$ first encountered peaches with olive oil in the Abruzzo region at the home of an olive grower. He wanted us to taste his olive oil, and since his garden tomatoes were not quite ripe, he sliced up some peaches instead. When I expressed my surprise at how good it tasted, he invited me to return when the tomatoes were ripe so that I could try his wife's summer salad of peaches, tomatoes, and creamy burrata cheese drizzled with the olive oil and sprinkled with fresh basil.

I have not been able to return yet, but in my own kitchen, I made this version with ripe summer peaches and juicy tomatoes. The colors are beautiful, and the flavor is spectacular.

Burrata is a fresh cow's-milk cheese similar to fresh mozzarella, but with a soft, creamy center. If you can't find burrata, see Sources (page 316) or substitute mozzarella.

Serves 4

3 firm but ripe peaches, pitted and cut into thin slices

2 ripe medium tomatoes, cut into thin slices

Coarse salt

8 ounces burrata or fresh mozzarella

12 fresh basil leaves, torn into bits

¼ cup extra-virgin olive oil

Alternate the peach and tomato slices on a platter. Sprinkle lightly with coarse salt.

Cut the burrata into chunks and place them in the center of the peaches and tomatoes. Scatter the basil on top, drizzle with the oil, and serve.

VARIATION

Substitute sliced ripe avocado or ripe figs for the peaches.

Chunky Vegetable and Cheese Salad

*M*y friend Louis Coluccio's grandmother used to make him this spicy salad for lunch. The vegetables came from a garden on the rooftop of his grandparents' Brooklyn home, which produced a bounty of tomatoes, chile peppers, and basil. Louis' grandmother would combine the vegetables with sharp provolone cheese and a zesty anchovy and lemon dressing and serve it over *friselle*, (hard bread rusks), or toasted crusty bread. Louis recommends a rich and full-flavored Southern Italian olive oil for the best flavor.

Serves 4

1–2 anchovy fillets, drained and chopped

¼ cup extra-virgin olive oil, plus more for drizzling

1–2 tablespoons fresh lemon juice

Salt and freshly ground pepper

3 large tomatoes, cut into bite-size pieces

2 hot cherry peppers, seeded and chopped

8 large fresh basil leaves, torn into bits

4 ounces imported Italian provolone, cut into small dice

4 *friselle* (see headnote) or 1-inch-thick slices Italian or French bread, toasted

In a medium bowl, using the back of a spoon, mash the anchovies together with the oil, lemon juice, and salt and pepper to taste.

Add the tomatoes, peppers, basil, and provolone to the bowl, and toss well. (Louis recommends using your hands.)

If using *friselle*, dip them briefly in cool water just to moisten. Break them up and place them in four salad bowls (or break up the toasted bread and put it in the bowls). Spoon the salad on top. Drizzle with a little more oil and serve.

Zucchini Carpaccio

In the height of summer, when zucchini is everywhere, this delightful preparation makes it seem like a whole new vegetable. Uncooked and sliced paper-thin, it is crisp yet tender. The dish tastes best when made with small (hot-dog size) zucchini, not the baseball-bat kind that can run rampant in the garden. Use green or yellow zucchini, or a combination of the two.

Fresh mint provides a refreshing accent, or you can substitute basil or parsley. Pecorino Toscano is not as sharp and salty as Pecorino Romano. It has a semi-firm texture and a mild nutty flavor that becomes stronger as it ages.

Serves 4

12 ounces small zucchini (about 5), scrubbed

2 tablespoons fresh lemon juice

2 tablespoons extra-virgin olive oil

Salt and freshly ground pepper

2 tablespoons chopped fresh mint or basil

A 2-ounce piece of Pecorino Toscano for shaving

Trim off the ends of the zucchini and cut into very thin slices. (A mandoline slicer or the thin slicer blade of a food processor does a good job.) Place the zucchini slices in a medium bowl.

Whisk together the lemon juice, olive oil, and salt and pepper to taste in a small bowl. Add the dressing and mint to the zucchini and toss well. Spread the zucchini on four plates.

With a vegetable peeler, shave the cheese into thin slices over the zucchini. Serve.

Zucchini Salad

*S*mall zucchini have much more flavor than the bland, pithy, oversized ones, and a simple fresh herb dressing is just the thing to complement them. Serve this salad with a frittata or as a side dish with chicken or spicy sausages.

Serves 4 to 6

Salt

1¼ pounds small zucchini (about 6), scrubbed

¼ cup extra-virgin olive oil

1 small garlic clove, grated (on a Microplane) or minced

2 tablespoons chopped fresh parsley

2 tablespoons chopped fresh basil

2 tablespoons chopped fresh mint

Bring a large saucepan of salted water to a boil. Add the zucchini and cook for 5 minutes, or until tender yet firm when pierced with a knife. Drain in a colander and cool under cold running water. Pat dry.

Trim the ends off the zucchini and cut them into thick slices.

In a medium bowl, toss the zucchini with the oil, garlic, and herbs. Add salt to taste and serve.

Arugula, Fig, and Pecorino Salad with Honey

I love how each bite of this salad has a variety of tastes and textures: crisp, nutty arugula, tender sweet figs, and salty cheese—all heightened with honey. A not-too-sharp cheese is perfect here, such as Pecorino Toscano or Parmigiano-Reggiano. Another way to go is crumbled fresh goat cheese.

When figs are out of season, make the salad with slices of ripe pears or Fuyu persimmons.

Serves 4

2 tablespoons extra-virgin olive oil

1 tablespoon red wine vinegar

Salt

2 bunches arugula, trimmed and torn into bite-size pieces (about 6 cups)

8–12 ripe figs, quartered

Freshly ground pepper

2 tablespoons honey

A 2-ounce piece of Pecorino Toscano for shaving

In a large bowl, whisk together the oil, vinegar, and salt to taste. Add the arugula and toss well.

Pile the arugula onto four serving plates. Garnish with the figs. Sprinkle with pepper to taste and drizzle with the honey. With a vegetable peeler, shave the Pecorino over all, and serve.

Arugula, Roasted Cremini, and Parmesan Salad

*A*rugula is easy to grow, even in a window box, so if you enjoy its flavor, consider growing it yourself. Here it teams up with roasted mushrooms and shavings of Parmigiano.

Serves 4

8 ounces cremini or white mushrooms, cleaned, trimmed, and quartered if large

¼ cup extra-virgin olive oil

Salt and freshly ground pepper

2 teaspoons balsamic vinegar, plus a few drops for drizzling

2 bunches arugula, trimmed and torn into bite-size pieces (about 6 cups)

A 2-ounce piece of Parmigiano-Reggiano for shaving

Preheat the oven to 425°F.

In a small baking pan, toss the mushrooms with 2 tablespoons of the oil and salt and pepper to taste. Roast until tender and lightly browned, about 15 minutes. Let cool slightly.

In a large bowl, whisk the remaining 2 tablespoons oil and the vinegar together with a pinch of salt and pepper to taste. Add the arugula and toss well.

Arrange the greens on four salad plates. Top with the mushrooms. Drizzle with a few drops of balsamic vinegar. With a vegetable peeler, shave some of the Parmesan over each salad, and serve.

Escarole Salad with Egg Mimosa

*W*hen many other vegetables are scarce in winter, escarole is at its best. The broad green and white outer leaves with paler yellow inner ones are chewy and slightly bitter. They are good cooked or raw in salads such as this one.

A sprinkling of grated hard-cooked eggs—called mimosa—adds a creamy texture and richness to this salad, which is dressed with an anchovy vinaigrette.

Serves 4

2 large eggs

12 ounces escarole, washed and trimmed

8 anchovy fillets, drained

¼ cup extra-virgin olive oil

2 tablespoons red wine vinegar

1 teaspoon Dijon mustard

Salt and freshly ground pepper

Place the eggs in a small saucepan with water to cover by 1 inch and bring to a boil over medium-high heat. Remove the pan from the heat, cover, and let stand for 12 minutes.

Drain the eggs and cool in cold running water. Crack and peel under running water.

Stack the escarole leaves a few at a time and cut them crosswise into 1-inch-wide strips.

In a large salad bowl, mash the anchovies to a paste with the back of a spoon. Whisk in the oil, vinegar, mustard, and salt and pepper to taste. Add the escarole and toss well.

Grate the eggs over the salad, using the large holes of a box grater. Serve.

Warm Potato Salad
with Bacon and Tomatoes

Crisp bacon, fresh basil, and sweet tomatoes enhance the flavor of this potato salad. I spotted something like it in an Italian cooking magazine, tinkered with the idea, and came up with this version. It's an excellent choice for a summer barbecue or as a companion to a frittata for brunch.

When I use onions raw in a salad, I like to soak them first in a bowl of cold water. This removes some of their sharp flavor and enhances their crunch. Be sure to pat them dry before adding them to the salad.

Serves 6

2 pounds waxy potatoes, such as Yukon Golds, scrubbed

1 medium red onion, thinly sliced

4 ounces bacon, cut crosswise into ½-inch-wide strips

1 large tomato, chopped

Salt and freshly ground pepper

⅓ cup extra-virgin olive oil

2 tablespoons red wine vinegar

⅓ cup shredded fresh basil

Place the potatoes in a saucepan with cold water to cover, cover, and bring to a boil. Cook for 20 minutes, or until the potatoes are tender when a knife is inserted in the center. Drain and let cool slightly.

While the potatoes are cooking, place the onion slices in a bowl of cold water, changing it once or twice.

Cook the bacon in a medium skillet over medium heat, stirring occasionally, until crisp and browned, 10 to 15 minutes. Remove the bacon with a slotted spoon and drain on paper towels.

Pour off all but 2 tablespoons of the fat from the skillet. Add the tomato and salt and pepper to taste and cook for about 4 minutes, stirring occasionally, until the tomato is softened slightly. Remove from the heat.

In a small bowl, whisk together the oil, vinegar, 1 teaspoon salt, and pepper to taste. Drain the onion and pat it dry.

Peel the potatoes and cut them into thick slices. Arrange a layer of potatoes on a serving platter. Sprinkle with some of the basil and drizzle with some of the dressing. Scatter some of the onion and tomato over the potatoes. Repeat the layering with the remaining ingredients. Scatter the bacon on top and serve.

Chickpea, Tomato, and Cucumber Salad

*P*anzanella is a classic Tuscan salad made with bread, tomatoes, onions, and other vegetables tossed with oil and vinegar. This salad is a variation on the theme, with chickpeas taking the place of the bread. Sometimes I garnish the salad with wedges of hard-cooked eggs or canned tuna for a simple summer meal.

Serves 4

1½ cups cooked chickpeas (see page 106) or one 16-ounce can chickpeas, drained

2 ripe medium tomatoes, cut into wedges

2 small Kirby cucumbers, peeled and sliced

½ small red onion, chopped

¼ cup chopped fresh parsley

3 tablespoons extra-virgin olive oil

1 tablespoon fresh lemon juice

Salt and freshly ground pepper

1 bunch arugula, trimmed (3 cups)

In a medium bowl, toss together the chickpeas, tomatoes, cucumbers, onion, and parsley. Drizzle with the olive oil and lemon juice, season with salt and pepper to taste, and toss well. Taste for seasoning.

Arrange the arugula on a platter. Top with the chickpea mixture and serve.

Herbed Green Bean and Potato Salad

My father used to love to go fishing in the waters off Sheepshead Bay in Brooklyn, where we lived. At home he would grill his catch while my mother prepared this salad, which is traditional in Southern Italy.

Serves 6

1¼ pounds waxy potatoes, such as Yukon Golds, scrubbed

Salt

8 ounces green beans, trimmed

½ cup chopped red onion

¼ cup extra-virgin olive oil

2 tablespoons red wine vinegar

Freshly ground pepper

¼ cup chopped fresh basil

¼ cup chopped fresh parsley

1 tablespoon chopped fresh dill

1 teaspoon chopped fresh thyme

Place the potatoes in a saucepan with cold water to cover, bring to a simmer, and cook until tender, about 20 minutes. Drain and let cool.

Meanwhile, bring a medium saucepan of salted water to a boil. Add the green beans and cook for 8 to 10 minutes, or until tender. Drain in a colander and cool under cold running water.

Pat the beans dry and cut them into 1-inch pieces.

Peel the potatoes and cut them into bite-size cubes. Transfer to a serving bowl and add the beans and onion.

In a small bowl, whisk together the oil, vinegar, and salt and pepper to taste. Whisk in the herbs. Pour the dressing over the vegetables, toss well, and serve.

Kale Salad with Fuyu Persimmons, Pine Nuts, and Pecorino

*K*ale as a salad green has been the star of any number of menus in the past few years—for good reason! Not only is it one of the healthiest greens, it's available year-round, tastes great, and, unlike other salad greens, doesn't wilt when it comes in contact with an acidic dressing. Though I've never eaten a kale salad in Italy, I decided to give the idea an Italian makeover by using typical ingredients like pine nuts and Pecorino cheese.

Fuyu persimmons are a delicious variety that does not have to be soft to be eaten. Unlike the more familiar dark orange Hachiyas, which are elongated and have a pointy bottom, Fuyus have a firm texture when ripe, similar to a mango. They are shaped somewhat like tomatoes and are yellow-orange. When persimmons are not in season, you can still make this salad: Just substitute another ripe fruit, such as oranges, pears, or apples.

Serves 4

1 pound kale, preferably Tuscan

2 ripe Fuyu persimmons, peeled

2 teaspoons Dijon mustard

1 tablespoon red wine vinegar

¼ cup extra-virgin olive oil

Salt and freshly ground pepper

¼ cup pine nuts, toasted

A 2-ounce piece of Pecorino Romano, Parmigiano-Reggiano, or imported Italian provolone for shaving

Trim the stems from the kale. Fold the leaves lengthwise in half and cut away the thick white center ribs. Stack the leaves a few at a time and cut them into ½-inch-wide ribbons.

Cut the persimmons into wedges, discarding the stems and seeds.

In a large bowl, whisk together the mustard, vinegar, oil, and salt and pepper to taste.

Add the kale and toss well.

Arrange the kale on four serving plates. Scatter the persimmons and pine nuts over the top. Shave the cheese over the salad and serve.

Radicchio and Grape Salad

*S*weet green grapes balance the slight bitterness of the radicchio in this salad, which I had in the Veneto region, where radicchio is an important crop. It adds bright color and a nice bite to salads and has the advantage of not wilting easily. If the grapes in the market don't look good, substitute a cut-up apple or pear or even orange wedges.

Serves 2

1½ tablespoons minced fresh parsley

1 tablespoon minced scallion

2 tablespoons extra-virgin olive oil

1 tablespoon honey

2 teaspoons white balsamic or apple cider vinegar

1 teaspoon Dijon mustard

Salt and freshly ground pepper

1 head radicchio (about 8 ounces), torn into bite-size pieces

1 cup halved seedless green grapes

In a small bowl, whisk together the parsley, scallion, oil, honey, vinegar, mustard, and salt and pepper to taste.

In a serving bowl, toss together the radicchio and grapes. Add the dressing and toss well. Taste for seasoning and serve.

Orange and Fennel Salad

*O*range salads are a favorite in Sicily, where every garden has at least one orange tree. They can be as simple as sliced oranges dressed with oil and salt and pepper or more elaborate like this one, in which anchovies provide a salty contrast to the sweet orange and crunchy fennel. It is a perfect starter for a fish dinner.

Serves 4 to 6

1–2 anchovy fillets, drained and chopped

2 tablespoons red wine vinegar

3 tablespoons extra-virgin olive oil

Salt and freshly ground pepper

1 small fennel bulb, trimmed and thinly sliced

¼ cup thinly sliced red onion

3 cups mixed baby greens

2 navel or blood oranges, peeled and sliced

¼ cup pitted imported oil-cured olives

In a small bowl, using the back of a spoon, mash the anchovies with the vinegar and oil. Whisk in salt and pepper to taste.

Place the fennel and onion in a medium bowl. Add half of the dressing and toss well.

Arrange the salad greens on a platter. Spoon the fennel mixture over the greens. Top with the orange slices and olives, drizzle with the remaining dressing, and serve.

Roasted Squash, Arugula, and Gorgonzola Salad

*C*hunks of roasted squash topped my big salad at ReCafé, a popular restaurant for young Romans. Roasting brings out the sweet flavor of the squash, and in this fall salad, it pairs well with crunchy apple slices, toasted walnuts, and peppery arugula.

Serves 4

2 cups cubed peeled butternut or other winter squash (about 8 ounces)

3 tablespoons extra-virgin olive oil

Salt and freshly ground pepper

1 tablespoon balsamic vinegar

2 bunches arugula, trimmed and torn into bite-size pieces (about 6 cups)

1 Gala or Golden Delicious apple, cored and thinly sliced

½ small red onion, thinly sliced

4 ounces Gorgonzola dolce, cut into bits

¼ cup walnut pieces, toasted

Preheat the oven to 425°F.

In a small baking dish, toss the squash with 2 tablespoons of the oil and salt and pepper to taste. Bake for 20 to 30 minutes, tossing once or twice, until tender and lightly browned. Let cool to room temperature.

In a small bowl, whisk together the remaining 1 tablespoon oil, the vinegar, and salt and pepper to taste.

In a large bowl, toss the arugula with the apple, onion, squash, and dressing. Pile the salad on four serving plates. Scatter the Gorgonzola and walnuts on top and serve.

Cookies, Cakes, and Tarts

Venetian Cornmeal Almond Cookies

*W*ith their nutty flavor and golden color, these little cookies are perfect to serve with tea or as an accompaniment to sorbet or ice cream for dessert. They are traditional in Venice, where they are known as *miottini*.

Makes about 5 dozen cookies

¾ cup almonds (with skins)

⅔ cup fine yellow cornmeal

1 cup unbleached all-purpose flour

¼ teaspoon salt

12 tablespoons (1½ sticks) unsalted butter, softened

1 cup sugar

3 large egg yolks

1 teaspoon grated lemon zest

Place the almonds and cornmeal in a food processor or blender and grind the almonds fine. Add the flour and salt and blend well.

In a large bowl, with an electric mixer on medium speed, beat the butter and sugar until blended. Add the yolks and lemon zest and beat until smooth. Beat in the dry ingredients.

Cover the dough with plastic wrap and chill for at least 1 hour, until firm.

Place racks in the upper and lower thirds of the oven and preheat the oven to 350°F. Line two large baking sheets with parchment or foil.

Pinch off a bit of the dough and shape it into a 1-inch ball. Place it on one of the baking sheets and flatten it slightly. Continue making the dough balls, placing them about 2 inches apart.

Bake the cookies for 15 to 20 minutes, or until lightly browned around the edges. Remove the pans from the oven and let cool for 5 minutes, then transfer the cookies to wire racks to cool completely.

The cookies can be stored for up to 1 week in a cool, dry place or frozen in plastic bags for up to 1 month.

Whole Wheat Biscotti
with Raisins and Walnuts

*W*hole wheat flour and walnuts give these cookies a hearty flavor, while raisins add mellow sweetness. With olive oil and other wholesome ingredients, these are one of the most healthful cookies. They keep well at room temperature in a covered tin and can also be frozen.

Makes 6 dozen biscotti

1½ cups unbleached all-purpose flour

1 cup whole wheat flour

1 teaspoon baking powder

1 teaspoon salt

1 teaspoon ground cinnamon

3 large eggs

1¼ cups sugar

1 cup extra-virgin olive oil

1 cup coarsely chopped walnuts

1 cup raisins

Place racks in the upper and lower thirds of the oven and preheat the oven to 325°F. Line two large baking sheets with parchment paper.

Whisk together the flours, baking powder, salt, and cinnamon in a medium bowl.

In a large bowl, beat together the eggs, sugar, and oil with a wooden spoon. Stir in the dry ingredients until evenly moistened. Add the walnuts and raisins and stir until blended. The dough will be soft.

Divide the dough into 4 pieces. Lightly moisten your hands and shape each piece into a 12-x-2-inch log. Place 2 logs 4 inches apart on each baking sheet.

Bake for 25 minutes, or until lightly browned. Remove the pans from the oven (do not turn it off). Let the logs cool for 10 minutes.

Slide the logs onto a cutting board one at a time. With a large heavy knife, cut each log diagonally into ½-inch-thick slices. Lay the slices about ½ inch apart on the baking sheets. Bake for 30 minutes, or until crisp. Cool the biscotti on wire racks.

The biscotti can be stored in a sealed container in a cool, dry place for up to 2 weeks or frozen in plastic bags for up to 1 month.

Rustic Fruit Focaccia

*D*uring the harvest season in Tuscany, very ripe wine grapes are used to make this delicious focaccia. It's good with other fruits too, such as peaches or blueberries. Although it is made with yeast, it isn't necessary to knead the dough—just stir it until a dough forms or beat it with an electric mixer.

Because it is not very sweet, I like to serve the focaccia as a breakfast bread or with afternoon tea. It is also good with a glass of Vin Santo or other dessert wine.

Serves 8

1 package active dry yeast

1 cup warm water (105°–115°F)

3 cups unbleached all-purpose flour

¼ cup sugar

2 teaspoons salt

⅓ cup extra-virgin olive oil

3 cups mixed ripe fruit, such as blueberries and sliced nectarines or apricots or peeled peaches (about 1 pound)

In a small bowl, sprinkle the yeast over the warm water. Let stand for 1 minute, or until creamy. Stir until dissolved.

In a large bowl, stir together the flour, 2 tablespoons of the sugar, and the salt. Add the yeast mixture and olive oil and stir with a wooden spoon until a moist, sticky dough forms.

Oil a large bowl. Add the dough, turning once to oil the top. Cover with plastic wrap and let rise in a warm, draft-free place until doubled in bulk, about 1½ hours.

Oil a 17-x-12-x-1-inch baking sheet. Place the dough on the pan. Oil your hands and gently flatten the dough out to fill the pan. Cover with plastic wrap and let rise until doubled in bulk, about 45 minutes.

Place a rack in the center of the oven and preheat the oven to 375°F.

Uncover the dough and scatter the fruit evenly over the surface, pressing the pieces in lightly. Sprinkle with the remaining 2 tablespoons sugar.

Bake for 30 to 35 minutes, or until the focaccia is lightly browned and crisp. Serve warm.

Polenta Berry Cake

orn is not native to the European continent. Historians say that it first arrived in Italy through Venice, a major shipping port, sometime after Columbus returned from the Americas. It was cheaper and easier to grow than wheat and soon became widely cultivated. Dried and ground into meal, it remains popular in the Veneto region, where it is cooked into polenta or added to cakes and cookies (see page 274).

Cornmeal adds a pleasant grainy texture and warm golden color to this cake. I have often enjoyed it plain, but one day I decided to add some berries to the batter, and I loved the result.

Serves 8

1 cup unbleached all-purpose flour

⅓ cup fine yellow cornmeal

1 teaspoon baking powder

½ teaspoon salt

12 tablespoons (1½ sticks) unsalted butter, softened

¾ cup plus 2 tablespoons sugar

1 teaspoon pure vanilla extract

½ teaspoon grated lemon zest

2 large eggs

⅓ cup whole milk

1 cup blueberries

1 cup raspberries

Place a rack in the center of the oven and preheat the oven to 350°F. Butter and flour a 9-inch springform pan. Tap out the excess flour.

In a large bowl, whisk together the flour, cornmeal, baking powder, and salt.

In a large bowl, with an electric mixer on medium speed, beat the butter until creamy, about 2 minutes. Gradually add ¾ cup of the sugar and beat until light and fluffy, about 3 minutes. Beat in the vanilla and lemon zest. Beat in the eggs one at a time, beating well after each addition and scraping down the sides of the bowl as necessary. On low speed, mix in half of the dry ingredients. Add the milk. Mix in the remaining dry ingredients just until smooth, about 1 minute.

Spread the batter in the pan. Scatter the berries over the top and sprinkle with the remaining 2 tablespoons sugar.

Bake for 45 minutes, or until the cake is golden brown and a toothpick inserted in the center comes out clean. Cool the cake in the pan on a wire rack for 10 minutes. Remove the pan rim and cool completely on the rack.

Cut the cake into wedges and serve, or cover and store at room temperature for up to 24 hours.

Clementine Upside-Down Cake

*T*here is something magical about upside-down cakes, known as *torte rovesciate* in Italy. When the baked cake is flipped over, it is drenched in the flavor of whatever fruits were in the bottom of the pan. Pineapple upside-down cakes are popular with Italians, as are those with figs, pears, peaches, and apples. This one is made with clementines, which are a type of mandarin orange. Use a serrated bread knife to cut them into thin, even slices.

This cake is at its best when served warm. A scoop of vanilla ice cream is the perfect accompaniment.

Serves 8

Topping

5 or 6 medium clementines

¾ cup packed light brown sugar

4 tablespoons (½ stick) unsalted butter, melted

Cake

1½ cups unbleached all-purpose flour

1½ teaspoons baking powder

½ teaspoon salt

8 tablespoons (1 stick) unsalted butter, softened

⅔ cup granulated sugar

1 teaspoon pure vanilla extract

2 large eggs

½ cup whole milk

Place a rack in the center of the oven and preheat the oven to 350°F. Butter a 9-inch round cake pan.

To make the topping

Grate the zest from 1 clementine and set it aside for the batter. Save the fruit for another use. Trim off a thin slice from the top and bottom of each of the remaining clementines. With a serrated bread knife, cut them crosswise, peel and all, into very thin slices; you should have enough to cover the surface of the cake. Remove the seeds.

Stir together the brown sugar and melted butter in a small bowl until the sugar is moistened. Spread the mixture evenly in the cake pan. Arrange the clementine slices, overlapping them slightly, on top.

To make the cake

In a medium bowl, stir together the flour, baking powder, and salt.

In a large bowl, with an electric mixer on medium speed, beat the butter until light and creamy, about 2 minutes. Add the granulated sugar, vanilla, and the reserved zest and beat until fluffy. Add the eggs one at a time, beating well after each addition and scraping down the sides of the bowl as necessary. On low speed, mix in half of the dry ingredients. Blend in the milk. Add the remaining dry ingredients and mix just until blended.

Spoon the batter into the pan and carefully spread it evenly over the fruit. Bake for 30 to 35 minutes, or until a toothpick inserted in the center comes out clean. Cool the cake for 10 minutes on a wire rack.

Run a small knife around the edges of the pan to loosen the cake, invert onto a serving platter, and carefully remove the pan. Let the cake cool to warm or room temperature before serving.

Hazelnut Cake with Chocolate-Espresso Sauce

*I*n Piedmont, I visited the area that grows the region's best hazelnuts. Naturally, I wanted to buy some nuts to bring home with me, but I was surprised to find that no one would sell them. When I asked why in one shop, the salesclerk said yes, she had some, but they were last year's crop and I should come back in a week or two when the fresh harvest was in. Sadly, I had to leave without them, though I did get to taste a number of wonderful desserts made with hazelnuts.

This cake is excellent plain with a cup of tea, but it is even better with the thick, creamy chocolate sauce—and maybe a scoop of vanilla ice cream.

Serves 8

Cake

1½ cups hazelnuts, toasted and skinned

½ cup unbleached all-purpose flour

½ teaspoon baking powder

½ teaspoon salt

8 tablespoons (1 stick) unsalted butter, softened

⅔ cup sugar

3 large eggs, at room temperature

Sauce

8 ounces bittersweet or semisweet chocolate, chopped

1 cup heavy cream

1 teaspoon instant espresso powder

To make the cake

Place a rack in the center of the oven and preheat the oven to 350°F. Butter a 9-inch springform pan.

In a food processor, finely chop the hazelnuts. Add the flour, baking powder, and salt and pulse just to blend.

In a large bowl, with an electric mixer on medium speed, beat the butter until light and creamy. Gradually add the sugar and beat until fluffy, scraping the sides of the bowl. Beat in the eggs one at a time, beating well after each addition. On low speed, beat in the dry ingredients just until blended.

Spread the batter evenly in the prepared pan. Bake for 30 minutes, or until a toothpick inserted in the center comes out clean. Cool the cake in the pan on a wire rack for 5 minutes.

Invert the cake onto a plate, then turn it right side up onto a rack to cool completely. (*The cake can be made up to 2 days ahead of time, covered with plastic wrap and refrigerated.*)

To make the sauce

Choose a heatproof bowl that can sit over a saucepan. Add water to the saucepan to a level that will not touch the bottom of the bowl, place the bowl over the saucepan, and bring the water to a simmer.

continued on page 284

Add the chocolate, cream, and espresso powder to the bowl and let stand for 5 to 10 minutes, or until the chocolate is softened. Stir until smooth. (*The sauce can be made ahead and refrigerated in an airtight container for up to 3 days; reheat gently.*)

Cut the cake into wedges and serve with the warm chocolate sauce.

Golden Apple Cake with Rum Cream

I first ate this cake in the Friuli-Venezia Giulia region of Italy, where it was served with Picolit, a golden dessert wine with a flavor like honey. Almost more apples than cake, it is topped with a dollop of rum-flavored whipped cream.

I usually use Golden Delicious apples, which are similar to the baking variety used in Italy. Sweet and juicy when raw, they hold their shape when cooked. Other good varieties for this cake include tart Granny Smith and crisp, juicy Jonagold.

Serves 6 to 8

Cake

9 tablespoons (1 stick plus 1 tablespoon) unsalted butter

3 medium Golden Delicious apples, peeled, cored, halved lengthwise, and cut crosswise into ¼-inch-thick slices

⅔ cup unbleached all-purpose flour

½ teaspoon baking powder

½ teaspoon salt

2 large eggs

1 large egg yolk

1 cup granulated sugar

1 teaspoon pure vanilla extract

½ teaspoon grated lemon zest

Confectioners' sugar

Whipped cream

1 cup heavy cream

2 tablespoons dark rum

To make the cake

Melt the butter in a large skillet. Pour 6 tablespoons of the butter into a large bowl.

Add the apples to the butter remaining in the skillet and cook over medium-low heat, stirring occasionally, until tender, about 10 minutes. Remove the pan from the heat and let cool slightly.

Place a rack in the center of the oven and preheat the oven to 375°F. Butter and flour a 9-inch round cake pan and tap out the excess flour.

In a medium bowl, whisk together the flour, baking powder, and salt.

Whisk the eggs and yolk, granulated sugar, vanilla, and lemon zest into the butter in the bowl. Beat in the dry ingredients with a wooden spoon. Fold in the apples.

Scrape the batter into the cake pan. Bake for 30 to 35 minutes, or until the cake is browned and puffed. Cool on a wire rack for 10 minutes.

Invert the cake onto a plate and lift off the pan, then invert the cake again onto the rack to cool completely.

To make the whipped cream

Place a large bowl and your mixer beaters in the refrigerator to chill.

Just before serving, pour the cream and rum into the chilled bowl and beat with an electric mixer on high speed until soft peaks form.

Sprinkle the cake with confectioners' sugar. Cut into wedges and serve with the whipped cream.

Plum Crostata

*S*weet-tart purple plums are the perfect fruit for this tart, though it also works well with peaches or apricots. You don't need to peel soft-skinned fruits. The cornstarch thickens the fruit juices so they form a natural glaze for the finished crostata.

Serves 8

Crust

1½ cups unbleached all-purpose flour

3 tablespoons sugar

½ teaspoon salt

1 teaspoon grated lemon zest

8 tablespoons (1 stick) cold unsalted butter, cut into bits

1 large egg, lightly beaten

1 teaspoon pure vanilla extract

Filling

8 large Italian prune plums or other large plums (about 2 pounds), pitted and quartered

½ cup sugar

2 tablespoons cornstarch

2 teaspoons fresh lemon juice

To make the crust

In a large bowl, stir together the flour, sugar, salt, and lemon zest. With a pastry blender or two forks, blend in the butter until the mixture resembles coarse meal.

Beat together the egg and vanilla in a small bowl. Drizzle the egg over the flour and toss with a fork until blended. Gather the dough into a disk, wrap in plastic wrap, and chill for at least 1 hour, or overnight.

Crumble the dough into a 9-inch tart pan. With your fingertips, pat the dough over the bottom and up the sides of the pan. Refrigerate for 30 minutes, or until firm.

Place a rack in the center of the oven and preheat the oven to 425°F. Place the tart pan on a baking sheet.

To make the filling

Toss the plums with the sugar, cornstarch, and lemon juice in a large bowl. Arrange the plums cut side up, overlapping slightly, in the pan.

Bake for 25 minutes. Reduce the heat to 375°F and bake for 25 to 30 minutes longer, or until the fruit is tender and the juices are bubbling.

Remove the pan from the oven. Dip a pastry brush in the juices and brush them over the fruit. Cool the tart on a wire rack for 30 minutes.

Remove the rim of the pan and let cool completely before serving.

Honey-Walnut Crumb Tart

*T*he melt-in-your-mouth crust and the crumb topping for this tart are made from the same dough. Cornstarch and plenty of butter are the secret to its tenderness. The fact that the crust is patted into the pan and not rolled makes it particularly easy. Sandwiched between the crust and crumbs is a rich honey and walnut filling that takes on a caramelized flavor as it bakes.

It is always a good idea to bake a tart on a baking sheet, especially when the filling is a loose one. That way, if the pan springs a small leak, it won't make a mess.

Serves 8

Crust and Crumbs

2 cups unbleached all-purpose flour

½ cup cornstarch

1 teaspoon baking powder

⅓ cup sugar

½ teaspoon salt

12 tablespoons (1½ sticks) cold unsalted butter, cut into bits

2 large egg yolks

1 teaspoon grated orange zest

About 3 tablespoons cold water

Filling

1½ cups walnuts

⅔ cup sugar

¾ cup heavy cream

2 tablespoons honey

To make the crust and crumbs

In a large bowl, stir together the flour, cornstarch, baking powder, sugar, and salt. With a pastry blender or two forks, blend in the butter until the mixture forms small crumbs.

Beat together the egg yolks, orange zest, and 3 tablespoons water in a small bowl. Pour the mixture over the flour and stir with a fork until it is evenly moistened. With your hands, pick up some of the dough and squeeze it until it holds together. If the dough is too dry, sprinkle it with up to 1 tablespoon of water. Repeat until the ingredients hold together and can be formed into a ball.

Set aside one quarter of the dough for the topping. Pat the remaining dough into the bottom and up the sides of a 9-inch tart pan. Refrigerate the tart pan and the reserved dough for at least 1 hour.

To make the filling

In a heavy saucepan, stir together the walnuts, sugar, cream, and honey. Cook over low heat, stirring occasionally, until the sugar has dissolved, about 10 minutes. Remove from the heat and let cool.

Place a rack in the center of the oven and preheat the oven to 375°F.

Place the tart pan on a baking sheet. Pour the cooled walnut filling into the tart shell. Crumble the reserved dough into crumbs and scatter them over the filling.

Bake the tart for 1 hour, or until the crumbs are golden brown. Cool on a wire rack for 20 minutes.

Remove the rim of the pan and let cool completely before serving.

Apricot and Mascarpone Tart

*A*fter a bowl of fresh pasta with zucchini and speck (a type of smoked ham) at Restaurant Ceci near Parma, followed by asparagus topped with butter, Parmigiano-Reggiano, fried eggs, and shaved black truffles, I didn't think I could eat another thing. I was about to request a cup of espresso when the waiter arrived bearing a freshly baked fruit tart. The filling, he said, was apricots and mascarpone, and the flavor, he added, was *squisito!* I took his recommendation and ordered a slice. The tart sweetness of the apricots and the creamy mild flavor of the mascarpone were heavenly. He was right—it was exquisite.

The tips of the golden apricot wedges peek out of the creamy filling, making this a beautiful dessert. Try it with peaches or plums when apricots are not in season.

Serves 8

Crust

1½ cups unbleached all-purpose flour

¼ cup sugar

½ teaspoon salt

1 teaspoon grated lemon zest

8 tablespoons (1 stick) cold unsalted butter, cut into bits

1 large egg

1 large egg yolk

1 teaspoon pure vanilla extract

To make the crust

In a large bowl, stir together the flour, sugar, salt, and zest. With a pastry blender or two forks, blend in the butter until the mixture resembles coarse meal.

Beat the egg, yolk, and vanilla extract in a small bowl. Drizzle the mixture over the flour and stir with a fork until incorporated.

Gather the dough together and shape it into a disk, then crumble it into a 9-inch tart pan. With your fingertips, pat the dough evenly over the bottom and up the sides of the pan. Refrigerate for 30 minutes, or until firm.

Preheat the oven to 375°F. Place the tart pan on a baking sheet.

Topping

8 ounces mascarpone, softened

1 large egg

3 tablespoons granulated sugar

1 teaspoon pure vanilla extract

5–6 apricots (about 1¼ pounds), pitted and cut into 4 wedges each

Confectioners' sugar for sprinkling

To make the topping

Whisk together the mascarpone, egg, 2 tablespoons of the sugar, and the vanilla. Spread the mixture in the tart shell. Place the apricot wedges skin side down into the mascarpone, pressing them in lightly. The ends will peek out of the cream. Sprinkle with the remaining tablespoon of sugar.

Bake for 60 to 70 minutes, or until the apricots are tender and the cream is set. Cool the tart on a wire rack for 30 minutes.

Remove the rim of the pan and let the tart cool completely. Just before serving, sprinkle with confectioners' sugar.

Pear and Almond Tart

*A*long, cold January afternoon of shopping the postholiday sales in Milan found my friend and me in need of a break. Lugging our shopping bags, we retreated to Sant Ambroeus, an elegant café named for the patron saint of Milan, and found it bustling with other exhausted shoppers. We ordered pots of hot tea and pastries from the gorgeous display cases. My choice was an individual tart with a classic combination of tender, buttery almond crust, creamy almond filling, and slices of sweet ripe pear. Soon we were refreshed and fortified, ready to face any shopping challenge.

Rather than making individual tarts, I bake this as a single tart large enough to serve eight. Anjou or Bartlett pears are my first choice here, though peaches or plums would be good when they are in season.

Serves 8

Crust

1 cup plus 3 tablespoons almonds (skin on), toasted

1½ cups unbleached all-purpose flour

¼ cup confectioners' sugar

½ teaspoon salt

8 tablespoons (1 stick) cold unsalted butter, cut into bits

1 large egg

1 large egg yolk

1 teaspoon pure vanilla extract

To make the crust

Place the almonds in a food processor and pulse until finely ground.

In a large bowl, stir together the flour, confectioners' sugar, salt, and 3 tablespoons of the ground almonds (reserve the remaining almonds for the filling). With a pastry blender or two forks, blend in the butter until the mixture resembles coarse meal.

Beat together the egg, yolk, and vanilla in a small bowl. Drizzle the egg over the flour and toss with a fork until blended.

Pat the dough evenly over the bottom and up the sides of a 9-inch tart pan. Refrigerate for at least 1 hour, or overnight.

Place a rack in the center of the oven and preheat the oven to 375°F. Place the tart pan on a baking sheet.

Filling

6 tablespoons (¾ stick) unsalted butter, softened

⅓ cup granulated sugar

2 large eggs

1 teaspoon pure vanilla extract

¼ teaspoon almond extract

¼ cup unbleached all-purpose flour

3 medium pears, such as Anjou or Bartlett

Confectioners' sugar for sprinkling

To make the filling

In a large bowl, with an electric mixer on medium speed, beat the butter and granulated sugar until blended. Add the eggs and the vanilla and almond extracts and beat well. Fold in the reserved ground almonds and the flour until smooth.

Spread the filling evenly in the tart shell.

Peel the pears and cut them lengthwise in half. Remove the cores and cut them crosswise into ¼-inch-thick slices, holding the slices together to keep the pear shape. With a metal spatula, slide the sliced pear halves onto the filling, with the narrow end toward the center of the tart. Press on the slices to fan them slightly.

Bake the tart for 45 to 50 minutes, or until the filling is golden brown. Cool the tart on a wire rack for 10 minutes.

Remove the rim of the tart pan and let the tart cool completely. Just before serving, sprinkle with confectioners' sugar.

Fruits, Spoon Desserts, and Ices

Berry Salad

A simple marinade of jam and lemon juice perks up even the most lackluster berries. Spike this salad with a little liqueur, if you like. Serve it plain or topped with ice cream or alongside cake.

Serves 4

3 tablespoons apricot jam

2–3 tablespoons fresh lemon juice

1 tablespoon orange liqueur, such as Grand Marnier or Cointreau (optional)

1½ cups sliced strawberries

½ cup raspberries

½ cup blackberries

½ cup blueberries

In a medium bowl, whisk together the jam, lemon juice, and liqueur, if using. Add the fruit and stir gently to coat. Let stand for 30 minutes before serving.

VARIATION

Substitute raspberry or blackberry jam for the apricot and cherry liqueur for the orange.

Red Wine–Poached Figs

*T*he season for fresh figs is brief, but if you are fortunate enough to have access to a fig tree, you know how abundant the harvest can be. They all seem to ripen at once!

I have tried growing figs on my terrace, not very successfully, but the local fruit vendors have plenty to sell, and I can't resist bringing them home by the boxful. They are good plain, wrapped in prosciutto, or stuffed with Gorgonzola. When they are less than perfect, I poach them in this simple red wine syrup to serve with plain cake or topped with a scoop of yogurt.

Serves 2

1 cup dry red wine
⅓ cup sugar
A 2-inch strip of lemon zest
8 ripe figs

In a medium saucepan, bring the wine, sugar, and lemon zest to a simmer over medium heat and stir to dissolve the sugar. Add the figs, cover, and cook for 10 minutes, or until tender when pierced with a knife.

Remove the figs with a slotted spoon and transfer to a bowl. Turn up the heat and boil the syrup for 5 minutes, or until slightly thickened. Pour the syrup over the figs. Let cool slightly and serve warm, or refrigerate and serve chilled. (*The figs can be made up to 3 days before serving and refrigerated in a covered container.*)

Raspberry-Poached Pears

oaching pears in white wine flavored with raspberries tints them a lovely pink. Light and refreshing, this dessert is also a treat for the eyes.

Serves 6

1 cup fresh or frozen raspberries

¾ cup sugar

A 2-inch strip of lemon zest

2 cups dry white wine

6 firm ripe pears, such as Bartlett, peeled

Whipped cream and raspberries for garnish (optional)

In a deep wide skillet, combine the raspberries, sugar, lemon zest, and wine and bring to a simmer over medium-low heat, stirring until the sugar dissolves, then simmer for 10 minutes.

Add the pears to the skillet, laying them down in the syrup. Cover and cook, basting and turning the pears once or twice, until they are tender when pierced in the thickest part, about 10 minutes. Transfer the pears to a shallow bowl, standing them upright.

Strain the syrup, pressing down on the solids to extract the liquid, and pour the syrup over the pears. Refrigerate until thoroughly chilled. (*The pears can be made up to 3 days ahead, covered with plastic wrap, and refrigerated.*)

Place the pears on serving dishes. Drizzle with the syrup. Garnish with whipped cream and fresh berries, if desired, and serve.

Honey-Roasted Plums

*T*ender plum halves glazed with honey and orange juice make a dessert as simple as it is elegant. The sauce thickens slightly as it cools. Serve these plain or with mascarpone, whipped cream, or yogurt.

Serves 4

4 medium red plums or 8 prune plums, halved and pitted
2 navel oranges
¼ cup honey

Preheat the oven to 375°F.

Place the plums cut side down in a baking dish just large enough to hold them in a single layer.

Peel off a 3-inch strip of zest from 1 orange. Cut the oranges in half and squeeze the juice into a small bowl. There should be about ¾ cup. Stir in the honey. Pour the liquid over the plums. Add the orange zest.

Bake the plums, basting every 10 minutes, for 30 minutes, or until tender when pierced with a knife. Let cool slightly and serve warm.

Warm Caramelized Fruit

*O*ne day I bought some nectarines that looked delicious, but when I tried one, it was cottony and flavorless. Disappointed, I was tempted to throw out the whole batch, but I decided to try to duplicate something I'd seen a cook make in Abruzzo, in central Italy.

I tossed the sliced nectarines and a handful of berries with rum and roasted them until they softened. Then I sprinkled on some sugar and roasted them a little longer, until the juices had caramelized.

It was magic! The sugar, rum, and fruit juices combined to form a luscious sauce, and the nectarines had become sweet and juicy. We ate the fruit warm with ice cream and the leftovers cold with yogurt. This also makes a good sauce for cake or a tasty topping for fresh ricotta for breakfast.

Use whatever fruits you like, such as nectarines, peaches, grapes, plums, berries, and apples. You will need about 8 cups of fruit in all.

Serves 6

5 large nectarines or peeled peaches, pitted and cut into wedges

6 medium apricots, pitted and cut into wedges

1 cup raspberries or blueberries

¼ cup dark rum or amaretto

¼ cup sugar

Vanilla ice cream or Greek yogurt (optional)

Preheat the oven to 400°F.

Place the fruit in a 13-x-9-x-2-inch baking pan and drizzle with the rum. Cover the pan with foil. Bake for 10 minutes, or until the fruit is tender when pierced with a fork (firm fruit such as apples will take longer).

Sprinkle the fruit with the sugar. Leave uncovered and return the pan to the oven. Bake for 10 to 15 minutes, or until the juices are thickened and slightly caramelized. Watch carefully so that the juices do not scorch.

Serve warm, plain or with ice cream, if you like.

Roasted Fruit Crunch

*A*crunchy amaretti cookie topping covers an assortment of fruit flavored with marmalade and orange juice. Vary the fruit according to the season or what you have on hand, but the amaretti are essential. Their superior crunch and deep almond flavor make them an ever-present ingredient in my pantry.

Serves 4

1 large apple, peeled, cored, and sliced

1 large pear, peeled, cored, and sliced

1 cup halved seedless red or green grapes

1 cup raspberries or blueberries

¼ cup orange marmalade

¼ cup orange juice

6 amaretti cookies, coarsely crumbled (about ⅓ cup)

1 tablespoon sugar

1 tablespoon unsalted butter

Preheat the oven to 375°F. Butter a 2-quart baking dish.

Scatter the fruit in the baking dish. (You should have about 5 to 6 cups.) Stir together the marmalade and orange juice and spoon the mixture over the fruit.

Toss the cookie crumbs and sugar together and sprinkle over the top of the fruit. Dot with the butter. Bake for 35 to 40 minutes, or until the fruit is tender. Let cool slightly before serving.

Two-Berry Tiramisu

*T*iramisu is usually made with chocolate and espresso, but I like this berry version even better. The colors are beautiful, and the rich mascarpone cream and berries complement each other wonderfully.

Italian-style ladyfingers are widely available in supermarkets and stores that stock Italian products, but the softer American ladyfingers can be substituted, as can slices of plain cake.

Serves 8

2 pints strawberries, hulled

1 pint raspberries

½ cup orange juice

¼ cup orange liqueur, such as Grand Marnier or Cointreau

¼ cup sugar

8 ounces mascarpone

1 cup heavy cream

24 savoiardi (Italian-style ladyfingers)

Set aside 2 cups of the best-looking strawberries for garnish. Chop the remainder. In a large bowl, combine the raspberries and chopped strawberries with the orange juice, liqueur, and sugar. Let stand at room temperature for 1 hour.

Scoop the mascarpone into a large bowl.

In a large chilled bowl, using chilled beaters, whip the heavy cream until soft peaks form when the beaters are lifted. Fold about one third of the whipped cream into the mascarpone to lighten it. Gently fold in the remaining whipped cream.

Layer 12 of the ladyfingers in a 9-x-9-x-2-inch glass baking dish. Spoon on half of the macerated berries and their juice. Spread half of the mascarpone cream over the berries. Repeat with a second layer of the remaining ladyfingers, berries, and cream. Cover and refrigerate for 3 to 4 hours, or overnight.

Just before serving, slice the reserved strawberries and arrange them in rows on top of the tiramisu. Cut into squares and serve.

Peach Cremolata alla Panna

*R*omans call this type of frozen fruit dessert *cremolata* because the milk gives it a slight creaminess, but it is not as creamy as gelato. I like to serve it the way they do in Italy—*alla panna*—topped with softly whipped unsweetened cream.

Serves 8

½ cup sugar
½ cup water
2 pounds ripe peaches
1 cup whole milk
1 cup heavy cream

Stir together the sugar and water in a small bowl. Let stand for 3 minutes, then stir until the sugar is dissolved.

Bring a pot of water to a boil. Add the peaches one or two at a time, then remove after 1 minute and let cool.

Peel the peaches, cut into chunks, and remove the pits. Place the fruit in a food processor or blender and blend until smooth. Add the sugar syrup and milk and process to blend. Pour into a bowl, cover, and refrigerate until chilled, at least several hours, or overnight.

Freeze the mixture in an ice cream maker according to the manufacturer's instructions. Scoop the *cremolata* into a covered container and freeze until firm, about 2 hours, or up to overnight.

Chill a large bowl and your mixer beaters in the refrigerator. Let the *cremolata* sit at room temperature for 10 to 15 minutes before serving.

Meanwhile, just before serving, add the cream to the chilled bowl and whip on medium-high speed with an electric mixer until soft peaks form.

Scoop the *cremolata* into goblets and top with the cream.

Almond Cremolata

*W*hen I was growing up in Brooklyn, a special Sunday treat was a trip to our favorite Italian bakery for almond *cremolata*, the frozen almond-flavored ice cream treat. It is hard to find almond *cremolata* in bakeries today, but it is easy to make it yourself at home.

Serves 6

4 cups whole milk

1 cup sugar

1 teaspoon pure vanilla extract

¼ teaspoon almond extract

½ cup almonds (with skins), toasted and coarsely chopped

In a medium saucepan, combine 1 cup of the milk and the sugar and cook over medium-low heat, stirring, until the sugar dissolves.

Pour the mixture into a large bowl. Stir in the remaining 3 cups milk and the vanilla and almond extracts. Cover and refrigerate until chilled, at least several hours or overnight.

Freeze the mixture in an ice cream maker according to the manufacturer's instructions. When the *cremolata* is almost ready, add the chopped almonds. Scoop the *cremolata* into a container, cover, and freeze until firm, about 2 hours, or up to overnight.

Let the *cremolata* sit at room temperature for 10 to 15 minutes before serving.

Lemon-Almond Semifreddo

$\mathcal{L}$emon zest, toasted almonds, and crunchy amaretti cookies are the flavoring for this gorgeous dessert, a kind of frozen mousse that is perfect for a party, since it can be made ahead of time. It's called *semifreddo*, meaning "half cold," because the whipped cream and egg whites keep it light and airy rather than frozen solid. The texture is enhanced by the addition of the crushed cookies and nuts.

There are many ways to vary this semifreddo, with chocolate cookies, hazelnuts, and orange zest, for example. Or change its appearance by freezing the mixture in a cake pan, bowl, or pretty mold, or make individual servings in custard cups. Instead of the fresh strawberries, serve the semifreddo with a caramel, chocolate, or fruit sauce.

Serves 8

2 cups heavy cream

1 cup confectioners' sugar

1 teaspoon grated lemon zest

⅛ teaspoon ground cinnamon

4 large egg whites

½ cup sliced almonds (with skins), toasted

1 cup coarsely crushed amaretti cookies

Strawberries for garnish

Line a 6-cup loaf pan or other mold with plastic wrap, leaving a 2-inch overhang all around. Chill the pan in the freezer.

In a large chilled bowl, using chilled beaters, whip the cream with an electric mixer until it thickens slightly. Add the confectioners' sugar and whip until soft peaks form when the beaters are lifted, 4 to 5 minutes. Beat in the lemon zest and cinnamon.

In a medium bowl, whip the egg whites with clean beaters until soft peaks form when the beaters are lifted.

Scoop about one quarter of the whipped cream into the bowl with the whites and fold gently with a rubber spatula until blended. Pour the mixture over the remaining whipped cream and fold it all together. Sprinkle with ¼ cup of the almonds and all of the crumbs and fold until blended.

Scrape the mixture into the prepared pan. Cover and freeze for at least 8 hours, or overnight.

To serve, unmold the semifreddo onto a serving dish. Peel off the plastic wrap and sprinkle with the remaining ¼ cup almonds. Cut into slices and garnish with strawberries.

Cherry Sorbet

When fresh fruit is not at its best, you can still make ices with fresh-picked flavor using frozen fruit. Serve this as is or paired with a scoop of vanilla frozen yogurt.

Serves 8

½ cup sugar

½ cup cold water

½ cup orange juice

½ teaspoon pure vanilla extract

¼ teaspoon almond extract

1 (16-ounce) bag frozen pitted dark sweet cherries

Stir together the sugar and water in a small bowl, let stand for 3 minutes, then stir until the sugar is dissolved. Stir in the orange juice and the vanilla and almond extracts.

Place the cherries in a food processor and coarsely chop. Add the orange juice mixture and process until smooth.

Freeze in an ice cream maker according to the manufacturer's instructions. Pack the sorbet into a container, cover, and freeze until firm, about 2 hours, or up to 3 days.

Let the sorbet sit at room temperature for 10 to 15 minutes before serving.

Pear and Grappa Sorbet

*A*ll the mellow floral flavor of ripe pears is captured in this elegant sorbet. I was served the sorbet as an intermezzo course at a fancy dinner years ago. I think it is much better for dessert. Grappa, a clear or golden spirit distilled from grapes, adds pizzazz, as does sprinkling a little more over the sorbet before serving.

Serves 8

1 lemon

1 cup sugar

1½ cups water

6 large ripe pears, peeled, halved lengthwise, and cored

2 tablespoons grappa

Remove a long strip of zest from the lemon, and squeeze the juice into a small bowl. In a large saucepan, combine the sugar and water, add the strip of zest, and bring to a simmer over medium heat, stirring until the sugar is dissolved.

Add the pears, cover, and cook over medium heat until tender when pierced in the thickest part with a knife, about 15 minutes. Remove from the heat and discard the lemon zest.

Remove the pears from the cooking syrup with a slotted spoon, transfer to a blender or food processor, and puree until smooth. Add the lemon juice and the syrup to taste to the pears and process until smooth. Add the grappa and process again. Pour into a bowl, cover, and refrigerate until chilled, at least several hours, or overnight.

Freeze the mixture in an ice cream maker according to the manufacturer's instructions. Pack into a container, cover, and freeze until firm, about 2 hours, or up to 3 days.

Let the sorbet sit at room temperature for 10 to 15 minutes before serving.

Red Wine and Blackberry Sorbet

$\mathcal{W}$ild blackberry bushes line the country roads in Italy, tempting passersby to brave the thorns and pick a basketful. Most of the berries are used for jam, but I was intrigued by this sorbet made with blackberries and red wine. Serve it with chocolate cookies for dessert.

Serves 8

1 cup sugar
1 cup dry red wine
12 ounces blackberries
2 cups water

In a medium saucepan, combine the sugar and wine and bring to a simmer over medium heat, stirring until the sugar is dissolved. Add the blackberries and water. When the liquid returns to a simmer, turn the heat down slightly and cook for 20 minutes, or until the blackberries are very soft. Let cool slightly.

Pour the mixture into a sieve set over a bowl. Press on the berries with a rubber spatula to extract all the liquid; discard the solids. Cover and refrigerate until chilled, at least several hours, or overnight.

Freeze the mixture in an ice cream maker according to the manufacturer's instructions. Pack into a container, cover, and freeze until firm, about 2 hours, or up to 3 days.

Let the sorbet sit at room temperature for 10 to 15 minutes before serving.

Watermelon Granita

*T*he only thing more refreshing than an icy-cold slice of watermelon on a hot summer's day is a cup of this granita. It captures the essence of the sweet juicy fruit and multiplies the flavor fivefold. Serve it with a small wedge of melon and a sprig of mint to enhance the effect.

Granita can be made in a shallow pan in your freezer, as instructed below, but you can also use an ice cream maker. It will have a smoother texture, more like sorbet, but it will still taste great.

Serves 6 to 8

6 cups seedless watermelon chunks

2 tablespoons fresh lemon juice

½ cup sugar

½ cup warm water

8 small wedges of watermelon and mint sprigs for garnish (optional)

In a food processor or blender, puree the watermelon, in batches if necessary, until smooth. Pour the puree into a bowl and stir in the lemon juice.

Stir together the sugar and water in a small bowl. Let stand for 3 minutes, then stir until the sugar is dissolved. Add the sugar syrup to taste to the pureed watermelon.

Pour the mixture into a shallow pan and freeze for 2 hours, or until ice crystals form around the edges. Scrape the frozen portion into the center and freeze for 30 minutes more. Stir again. Continue freezing and stirring until the granita is completely frozen, about 2½ hours. (*The granita can be stored, covered, in the freezer for up to 3 days.*)

Let the granita stand at room temperature briefly to soften slightly before serving. Garnish with the melon wedges and mint sprigs, if you like, and serve.

Olive Oil Gelato

*I*t may sound weird, but olive oil gelato is so creamy and luxurious that this recipe will undoubtedly enter your permanent repertoire. The flavor is subtle and elusive, yet totally delicious. It doesn't taste at all oily. Serve with fresh berries for a heavenly experience.

Serves 6 to 8

4 large egg yolks
½ cup sugar
2 cups whole milk
1 cup heavy cream
¼ cup extra-virgin olive oil
1 teaspoon pure vanilla extract

In a medium bowl, whisk together the egg yolks and sugar.

In a medium saucepan, heat the milk over low heat until small bubbles form around the edges. Gradually whisk the hot milk into the egg mixture. Pour the mixture back into the saucepan and cook over medium-low heat, stirring constantly with a wooden spoon, until the custard has thickened and wisps of steam appear on the surface, about 8 minutes.

Immediately pour the custard through a sieve into a bowl. Whisk in the cream, olive oil, and vanilla until well blended. Refrigerate until chilled, at least several hours or overnight.

Whisk the custard and freeze in an ice cream maker according to the manufacturer's instructions. Scoop the gelato into a container, cover, and freeze until firm, about 2 hours, or overnight.

Let the gelato sit at room temperature for 10 to 15 minutes before serving.

Strawberry-Mascarpone Gelato

*M*ascarpone, the thick cream cheese from Northern Italy, makes the richest gelato I have ever eaten. Garnish with a few perfect strawberries.

Serves 6 to 8

3 cups strawberries, hulled and quartered, plus several whole strawberries for garnish

¾ cup sugar

Pinch of salt

1 (8-ounce) container mascarpone cheese

1 cup whole milk

1 tablespoon fresh lemon juice

Place the quartered strawberries in a blender or food processor and puree until smooth. Pour the puree into a sieve set over a large bowl. Press on the berries with a rubber spatula to extract all the juices; discard the solids.

In the blender or food processor, combine the sugar, salt, mascarpone, milk, and lemon juice and blend until smooth. Pour the mixture into the strawberry puree and stir well. Cover and refrigerate until chilled, at least several hours, or overnight.

Freeze the mixture in an ice cream maker according to the manufacturer's instructions. Scoop the gelato into a container, cover, and freeze until firm, about 2 hours or overnight.

Let the gelato sit at room temperature for 10 to 15 minutes before serving. Garnish with the whole strawberies and serve.

Sources

Dried Beans

www.republicofbeans.com

www.dipaloselects.com

**Mozzarella, Burrata, Parmigiano-Reggiano,
Fontina Valle d'Aosta, and other Italian cheeses**

www.dipaloselects.com

www.murrayscheese.com

www.eataly.com

**Canned Italian Tomatoes, Capers, Olives, Olive Paste,
Pasta, Anchovies, Bottarga, Jarred Chestnuts**

www.dipaloselects.com

www.eataly.com

www.olioandolive.com

www.amazon.com

Truffles, Truffle Butter

www.eataly.com

www.urbani.com

Index